On the Grid

ON THE GRID

Australian Electricity in Transition

Edited by Guillaume Roger

MONASH
UNIVERSITY
PUBLISHING

On the Grid: Australian Electricity in Transition

Monash University Publishing
Matheson Library Annexe
40 Exhibition Walk
Monash University
Clayton, Victoria 3800, Australia
publishing.monash.edu/

Monash University Publishing: the discussion starts here.

ISBN: 9781922633217 (paperback)
ISBN: 9781922633224 (pdf)
ISBN: 9781922633231 (epub)

Design: Les Thomas
Typesetting: Jo Mullins

A catalogue record for this book is available from the National Library of Australia.

Contents

Preface

Rightly or wrongly, in our federation, the energy transition is occurring – with or without the federal government. While engineering solutions arise to assist with this transformation, the institutions governing the electricity market are failing to adjust rapidly enough to the new energy mix and to the demands on the power system. This precarious situation is further impaired by hangovers from the era of deregulation gone wrong. The results are institutional sclerosis and some of the highest electricity prices in the world in spite of an abundance of energy. None of this is inevitable; like all institutions, it is all man-made.

This volume is an edited collection of essays, each of which is based on informed academic research. The purpose of this book is to draw attention to the dire need for deep market reforms to accommodate, and take advantage of, the rapid energy transition Australia is experiencing. It points to problems and asks questions, thereby laying out a vast program of policy formulation. The energy transition is so far-reaching that some of the fundamental work required to underpin these yet-to-be-formulated policies remains to be done. We suggest it is high time to get started.

These essays are, purposefully, written much less formally than academic research but are nonetheless based on rigorous work. They are somewhat disjointed but collectively they paint a cohesive picture. By no means do we claim this book to be exhaustive of the issues; if it is a starting point, we have succeeded.

The reader should fittingly begin with the first chapter, by David Havyatt, which presents a historical perspective of the evolution of the power sector in this country. It shows this industry to be in a constant state of flux, and so suggests first we should accept this reality; there simply is no perfect solution, especially in the decentralised environment that Australia embraced in the 1990s. It also documents a clear need for coordination (of power flows, of energy generation, of transmission investment) that is the hallmark of a modern power system, for it is the only way to take care of the many externalities a power network entails.

To continue with a (more recent) historical account, the reader may then move on to the contribution by Stephen King, who covers transmission reforms. King suggests transmission assets are not necessarily natural monopolies, which must therefore be regulated. At least some transmission links may be open to competition, especially if transmission operators are allowed to participate in congestion pricing and congestion management – possibly under some form of regulatory supervision.

Chapter 3, by Steve Callander, sheds light on the pitfalls of backsliding – the phenomenon whereby competition first introduced by deregulation is progressively curtailed by increasing concentration thanks to political support. This is not unique to electricity, nor to Australia, but is evidently an accurate depiction of the present situation, which so many commentators bemoan. Callander not only uncovers the important, and widely relevant, nexus of regulation and political interference, he also offers avenues to escape the morass of backsliding.

The last two chapters are more specific to the electricity sector, and more forward looking. In Chapter 4, Orrie Johan, Gordon Leslie, Tom Meares and Russell Pendlebury make the case for a major reform of market design. Nodal pricing, long in use in the United States, offers more arbitrage opportunities for storage operators, without whom there is simply no energy transition.

In the final chapter, Guillaume Roger gives an overview of the current state of the wholesale market and suggests a concrete agenda for reforms that includes market design, considerations of competition policy and giving a role to the demand side.

Taken together, these contributions suggest an ambitious reform agenda that spans governance, wholesale market, transmission and competition policy. Just like large banks may be too big to fail, ambitious reforms are often too big to get up. In this instance, however, the technological shift supplies the impetus for reform. The rents of incumbents are dissipating in front our eyes, and consumers and states take matters in their own hands. This makes for an opportune time for profound reforms.

Guillaume Roger
February 2022

Chapter 1

History of Electricity Reform in Australia

David Havyatt[1]

1. Introduction

Being mindful of the dictum 'Those who cannot remember the past are condemned to repeat it' (Santayana 1905–06), the analysis of electricity market reform needs to place the reforms themselves in their historical economic context. History isn't, however, just a 'corpus of ascertained facts'; the historian chooses the facts that are significant to them and the analysis they wish to provide.[2]

Many articles on the Australian market include some short references to history. Rai and Nelson (2019) are not atypical in their opening to a review of twenty years of Australia's National Electricity Market when they write:

> Prior to the 1990s' Hilmer microeconomic reforms, the east-coast Australian electricity industry's functions – generation, transmission and distribution, and retail supply – were vertically integrated within government owned state electricity commissions. Following the reforms, the competitive components (electricity generation and retailing) were separated from those with monopoly characteristics (transmission and distribution).

---

1   **David Havyatt**, PhD Candidate, School of Business, Faculty of Business and Law, University of Wollongong, NSW.
      The author would like to thank Simon Ville, John Quiggin and Guillaume Roger for their comments and suggestions on earlier drafts of this chapter.
2   Carr (1961), who also advises us that 'when we take up a work of history, our first concerns should be not with the facts which it contains but with the historian who wrote it'.

This shorthand division into two periods, first of vertically integrated state-owned enterprises and then of a structurally separated competitive market, suits any writer who wants to focus on that latter period. However, the issue becomes more extreme when writers talk about a period of 'unprecedented change'.[3] This history will focus on the alternative view that change has been a constant in the electricity supply industry (ESI) and that the failure to understand the industry dynamics has led to some of the challenges now faced.

As Newbery and Green (1996, p. 26) note:

> The modern approach to the design of regulatory systems often overlooks the historical constraints placed on the options available for reform and implicitly assumes the state of the industry is one of neutral equilibrium, in which any displacement will not set in train a sequence of subsequent changes that have long-term implications for structure and performance of the industry.

Economists that policy makers and the industry engage are over endeared to equilibrium models rather than change; the approach to market design fails to consider how institutions will transition to a competitive market. One consequence has been the ongoing lack of significant demand-side participation over the twenty years after reform.

Engineers embedded in the system have also failed to incorporate the reality of change; their mode of thinking is determined by the technology or the 'regime' to use the term from the multi-layer perspective of socio-technical transitions (Geels 2002). As an example, the market operator (AEMO) is responding to issues of low minimum demand from high levels of solar PV connected to the distribution network only now that it has become a problem, rather than beforehand.[4]

The story told here is similar to the global experience, as detailed by Hausman et al. (2008). They emphasise the capital-intensive nature of the ESI and the role foreign capital often played in early developments. Increased government activity and ownership followed before coming full circle to the post-1980s and 1990s reforms, with growing ownership often by large multinational firms. The Australian narrative is slightly different, as we will

---

3   See, for example, Karmel (2018), Moran and Sood (2013), ENA and CSIRO (2016).

4   See AEMO's Renewables Integration Study Stage 1 Appendix A: High Penetrations of Distributed Solar PV: https://aemo.com.au/-/media/files/major-publications/ris/2020/ris-stage-1-appendix-a.pdf?la=en.

see, with governments taking a more active early role, but overall the arc of the story is consistent with their themes.

This history is divided into four sections. The first deals with the primarily municipal origins of the ESI. The second deals with the development of the State Electricity Commission model, which occurred at different times in each state from 1919 to 1950.

The third section covers the national market reforms that followed the inquiries by the Industries Assistance Commission (IAC 1989) and the Industries Commission (IC 1991). The complete analysis of the thirty years since the reports of 1989 and 1991 belongs in post-1945 economic history.[5] The 'micro-economic reform' of the ESI is a significant element of that research program; this, however, is but a small contribution to that study.

The final section will discuss briefly how this history should inform reformers, observing the gap between outcomes and objectives of reform.

The initial motivation for the ESI in Australia was a public safety issue of the provision of street lighting. The authorities established to provide the service rapidly expanded to provide businesses and households with electric lights and appliances. However, very early in this history, reliability of the supply became an issue, which was addressed first by the linking up of generators and municipal systems.

Other reliability concerns flowed from the availability of fuel, with two states establishing government entities to develop brown coal resources: the State Electricity Commission in Victoria in 1919 and Electricity Trust of South Australia in 1946 in South Australia. Tasmania, blessed with abundant water resources, established a Hydro-Electricity Department in 1914 (converted to a Commission in 1929) to exploit these to support a metallurgical industry. New South Wales (1950) and Queensland (1938) were motivated by realising the efficiencies of scale inherent in large centralised generation and the economic development of regional areas.

The Commission model was well established by the 1970s and continued to expand the footprint of the state grids when the focus turned from resource adequacy to oversupply and the reversal of at least three decades of steadily

---

5   McLean and Shanahan (2007) report that three themes have emerged as important new directions for Australian Economic History – a focus on post-1945 economic issues, a consideration of the history of economic policies and a move from macro-economic growth focus to 'micro dimensions of that story'. Economics and economists have been increasingly relied upon since WWII in determining government policy and it identifiably falls in two periods – postwar Keynesianism and then neoliberal 'microeconomic reform'.

declining electricity prices. The oversupply crisis and poor management decisions were the impetus for the reforms of the 1990s; the introduction of competition was secondary to the objective of building a national grid. At the same time, the new issue of greenhouse gases and their effect on the climate was being observed.

Despite the image of the 1990s reforms being pivotal, the earliest call for the Commonwealth Government to take an active role was the 1929 *Report on Power Development in Australia* (Gibson 1929). This report proposed that the government set up a 'suitable organisation' to control national waterways (for hydro-electricity), control electrical energy when transferred from one state to another, and ensure the standardisation and coordination of frequency, voltage and methods throughout Australia. That report also recommended that the Commonwealth assist states in every way possible to develop their power resources.

Once we accept that the system has been in a constant state of transition and reform as the technologies of generation, transmission and consumption changed, three trends become evident:

- The resistance to change by incumbent organisations, including municipal undertakings, state commissions or private sector businesses.
- The federal model of government failed to develop a coherent framework for developing and executing energy policy.
- As a consequence of the first two, a tendency to develop short-term solutions to long-term problems and an underestimation of how long it will take to develop and implement reforms.

These trends are masked in the dominant narrative of the history of the ESI as consisting of two periods (vertically integrated state-owned entities followed by structurally separated businesses in a national market separated by a single review). It makes the idea of further reform to address the changing nature of generation sound simple: a matter of just redesigning the markets and system using engineering and economics and implementing it through legislation and subordinate instruments.

Importantly the fundamental questions of reliability and technical efficiency resulting in the lowest costs have been present since the start. The additional challenges of demand management and emissions reduction identified in the 1990s also remain unresolved. Focusing on the system's evolution through to 2050, rather than the reforms needed to survive another decade, would at least provide an opportunity to consider the system's institutional environment and dynamic responses.

2.   Municipal origins

While electricity had been used for lighting in various individual uses, such as illuminations in Sydney to celebrate the wedding of the Prince of Wales in 1863 and a night football game at the MCG in August 1879 (Edwards 1969), the electricity supply industry in Australia dates from street lighting in Tamworth in 1888 (Tait 1925). The ESI is the generation of electricity in one place for consumption by one or more customers in multiple other locations. The first two uses were traction (tramways) and lighting (Butlin et al. 1982, p. 282). To realise economies of scale and level-out demand, tramways and railways sold bulk power to municipal undertakings and industry. At the same time, public lighting utilities marketed early household appliances, while they also commenced selling electric motors to factories.

There are valuable histories of the development of individual systems or localities.[6] While municipal supply was a common model across all countries, in Australia the involvement of municipal authorities almost always began through the provision of the public good of street lighting. In the USA, municipal authority involvement was more commonly authorising poles and wires through streets. That is not to say that there weren't also municipality-owned companies; they just weren't as prevalent.

---

6   This history draws on the major published studies for the regions included in the National Electricity Market. Queensland is well covered by a two-volume history of electricity in Queensland (Thomis 1987, 1990) and two studies of parts of regional Queensland (Doran 1990; Williams 1983). South Australia is also covered by two studies, one focused on the state utility after government took ownership (Linn 1996) and an unpublished doctoral thesis (Spoehr 2008). For Victoria there is a history published by the State Electricity Commission to commemorate its first fifty years (Edwards 1969), and in New South Wales two histories (in part) of Sydney commissioned originally by what became of the Sydney County Council (Darroch 2015; Wilkenfeld 2004) and an unpublished thesis detailing the history of the Electricity Commission (Thornton 2015).

Other histories include ones for various NSW municipalities (Armstrong 2002; Inchbold-Busby 2011; Low 1992, 2004; Wilkenfeld 2004), for Qld (Board 1977; Morwood 1968; Pearson 2000, 2001, 2007, 2010; Prentice 1982; Smith 1988), for SA (Kerr and Kerr 1979; McLaren 1994), for Victoria (Andersen 1992; Dike and Lamb 2012; Harvey and Peckman 1993; Lincolne 1955; Napier and Easdown 1993; Penrose 1995; Ruddock 1981; Rusden 1968; Society 2003; Vines 2000; White 1986), for Tasmania (Garvie 1962; Read 1985) and the ACT (Jones 1980).

Our history and geography shaped a different role of government in Australia compared to the UK and USA. As Quiggin (1996) notes, three factors motivate this difference. The first is Australia's origins as a penal colony where, almost by definition, the government delivered the whole society's needs. The second is Australia's development of democratic government without revolution or force, so the government is not primarily seen as a power to be feared. The third has been the geographic consequence of a vast, thinly populated land where only the government could raise the requisite finance for many projects.

Notwithstanding these factors, the extent of early private ownership of electricity utilities and electric powered transportation is often overlooked. In the case of Sydney, many municipalities were served by the Balmain Power Company. Other major private sector undertakings included The Adelaide Electric Supply Company Ltd; Kalgoorlie Electric Power and Lighting Corporation; Melbourne Electric Supply Company Ltd; Electric Supply Company of Victoria Ltd; Brisbane Electric Tramways Investment Company; Kalgoorlie Electric Tramways Ltd; and The North Melbourne Electric Tramway and Lighting Company Ltd. Consistent with Quiggin's observation, capital formation was locally challenging, and the listed private companies were listed on the London stock exchange.

Quiggin's three items are not the only factors that distinguish the Australian experience. Australian 'exceptionalism', that Australia has prospered by being a resource-rich nation while avoiding the typical problems of corruption, low growth or stagnation, has been attributed to the development of an adaptive framework of national institutions (McLean 2013). Though from a very different perspective on economics, Chester (2012) has advanced a similar position to explain why Australia was alone in the Anglophone neoliberal economies in avoiding recession following the Global Financial Crisis.[7]

We will not attempt a complete genealogy of all the enterprises that make up the ESI through history. Instead, we provide two simple case studies of municipal enterprises leading up to the formation of state authorities. The first is a review of the development of the ESI in Sydney, while the second is a short history of electricity in the Queensland country town of Longreach.

---

7   It is noted that the term Global Financial Crisis is a term mostly restricted to use in Australia; however, it is more descriptive than terms such as 'the crisis' or 'the great recession' used elsewhere.

The ESI in Sydney[8]

Tamworth installed street lighting in 1888, and by 1892 Young, Penrith, Moss Vale and Broken Hill had also done so. Newcastle soon followed. The small municipality of Redfern, adjacent to the Sydney Municipal Council, built a small power station to illuminate its main shopping area in 1891.

The NSW railways first generated electricity in 1893 for a trial tram route to Randwick. By 1902 the railways completed the construction of a power station at Harris Street in Ultimo (now the Powerhouse Museum) to supply power for the tramways, and the famous Bondi tram was travelling at speeds of 30km per hour (hence the colloquialism 'shoot through like a Bondi tram').

In Sydney, the Council's 'Electricity Undertaking' commenced operation in 1904. It initially faced five pre-existing electricity undertakings: Palace Electric Lighting, Strand Electric Lighting, Oxford Street Electric Lighting, Imperial Arcade Electric Lighting and Empire Electric Light. As their names suggest, these primarily lit shops and their surrounding precincts. After a period of price competition, the Undertaking acquired four in 1907 and the last, together with the Redfern Municipal Council power station, in 1913.

The Undertaking extended its service into other Sydney municipalities at their request (and cost) and by 1910 included Paddington, Annandale, Mascot, Randwick and Woollahra in its service area. Balmain Borough Council chose a private-sector approach and granted a franchise to the Electric Light and Power Supply Corporation.[9] This entity (popularly known as the Balmain Power Company) competed to serve councils and secured the right to supply Newtown, Leichhardt, Ashfield and Petersham. Progressively each added other council areas. The railways built a second power station at White Bay in 1911 though full electrification was not completed until 1926. Electricity supply in Sutherland, Bankstown and Campbelltown began in the early 1920s using bulk power supply from the railways.

Growth in demand, combined with delays in capacity expansion due to the First World War disrupting supply and the impact of the Great Strike in 1916, resulted in challenges for the Undertaking in providing capacity to meet demand. This supply challenge resulted in talks between the Railway Commissioners and the Undertaking about 'linking up' their mutual systems

---

8   This summary is mostly drawn from Darroch (2015) and Wilkenfeld (2004).

9   In 1903 Balmain Council had been directed by the Public Health Department to cease the open tip dumping of local rubbish. The Council called for tenders for a combined waste destruction and power generating facility. The power station burnt waste and coal.

and exchanging power from their respective power stations (Pyrmont and White Bay). As a result, they reached an interchange agreement in 1919.

In 1936 the Undertaking was removed from the control of the City Council after numerous cases of corrupt conduct. The new entity – the Sydney County Council – was governed by five councillors: two from the City of Sydney, two from the 25 municipalities south of the harbour, and one from the seven to the north.

Further difficulties for the Undertaking arose when the Second World War caused delays in equipment ordered from the UK. By this time, there were four generating authorities in the Sydney region. These were the SCC (with power stations at Pyrmont and Bunnerong), the Railways (White Bay), the Balmain system (the power station stood on the south side of Iron Cove beside the Iron Cove Bridge) and the Department of Public Works at Port Kembla.[10] As a wartime security measure, these four existing generating authorities linked up into a 'primitive electricity grid' – the SCC and Railways had, as noted, been connected since 1919.

Following the war, supply problems caused by failed equipment deliveries and coal strikes resulted in frequent blackouts. In response, and recognising the changing economics of generation and transmission, the NSW Government formed the Electricity Commission of NSW in 1950. It acquired the power stations and main transmission lines of the four foremost supply authorities: Southern Electricity Supply (the Port Kembla station), Sydney County Council, the Department of Railways and the Electric Light and Power Supply Corporation Ltd. The Commission was responsible for the centralised coordination of the state's electricity generation and supply, with separate distribution businesses providing consumer connections. There had been 188 electricity generation and distribution bodies in NSW in 1948. Following the creation of the Electricity Commission, consolidations reduced this to sixty-nine distribution businesses by 1959. By 1980 this reduced to twenty-six, all government-owned.[11]

The availability of hydro-generation from the Snowy Mountains Scheme for peak and emergency power enabled New South Wales to use large generating

---

10   This power station had been constructed to provide electricity for the construction of the harbour facilities.

11   The most common structure was a County Council which was a cooperative of city, municipal or shire councils. Wilkenfeld (2004) provides a table at Appendix 3 showing the history of the consolidation of the supplies in the areas served by EnergyAustralia in 2004 (this is now the area served by Ausgrid as a Distribution Network Service Provider).

plant as base-load units. As a result, according to Commissioner McDonnell, it became 'a world leader in the technologies of large black-coal generation' (Commission of Inquiry into Electricity Generation Planning in New South Wales 1987).

Longreach Powerhouse[12]

Sitting in the Central West of Queensland, 700km from the Eastern Coast, Longreach takes its name from the 'long reach' of the Thomson River on which it sits. The town was gazetted in 1887 as part of the railway development, which reached the town in 1892. In 1921 Longreach became the base for Queensland and Northern Territory Aerial Services Ltd (Qantas).

Also in 1921, electricity was first generated in the Longreach Powerhouse. Longreach Shire Council owned and operated the powerhouse from 1921 to 1966 to install an electric light scheme for the town. The service only supplied the main portion of the town until extending to residents in the eastern and northern portions in 1924. In later years the powerhouse supplied power to Longreach, Ilfracombe and Isisford, and a large rural grid.

From 1921 to 1943, the power station provided a DC (direct current) supply (32V) only. To transmit power over longer distances using AC (alternating current), the power station generated a dual supply of DC and AC from 1943 to 1953. As residents became aware of the advantages of 240V AC (primarily for more appliances), the Council received steady applications for conversion to AC. Work began to convert the whole supply to AC in 1953 and was completed in 1954.

The first engines were Ruston & Hornsby charcoal gas units powering DC generators by a belt drive. Timber was initially used as a fuel source because it was cheap to obtain and in plentiful supply. The timber was burnt, and the resulting charcoal was provided to the power station for use in the gas producers. Charcoal was used until the 1940s; after almost twenty-five years, timber of suitable quality became hard to come by and was no longer cheap.

In 1948 a National RA7 engine was installed, this being the first oil engine used to generate electricity in the powerhouse. It was installed as an interim measure due to the difficulty of sourcing charcoal and because the conversion to gas produced from coal would take some time to complete. It was also the first unit capable of generating AC power.

---

12   This history is entirely constructed from the information on display at the Longreach Powerhouse.

In 1966 the Central West Regional Electricity Board took over the operation of the power station. This new Board had responsibility for the supply of electricity in the Shires of Longreach, Barcaldine, Blackall, Tambo, Jericho, Aramac, Ilfracombe and Isisford. Power generation was centralised in Longreach and Barcaldine. A 66kV transmission line was constructed between Longreach and Barcaldine in 1973 to equalise generation supply between the two towns.

The powerhouse ownership was transferred to the Capricornia Electricity Board (CAPELEC) in 1977 following a reorganisation of the electricity industry. Generation continued in Longreach supplying electric power to Longreach, Ilfracombe, Isisford and Morella until 1985 when electric power was delivered to the region from the state grid via a transmission line which originated at the Gladstone Power Station.

In 1998 the 66kV line connecting Longreach to Barcaldine was replaced; the new line used concrete poles instead of the original wooden poles and took a route close to the Landsborough Highway. This significantly reduced faults on the line, which averaged over 25 power outages per year. As CAPELEC said at the time, 'the new transmission line takes into account the difficulties associated with supplying customers from long transmission, distribution and SWER [single-wire earth return] networks'.

Longreach is a classic outback town, initially developed in the second half of the nineteenth century and, throughout the twentieth century, struggling to get services to match those in the cities. The progress of electrification from charcoal-gas engines powering generation through to a modern grid connection using cheap centrally generated power from large coal-fired power plants was an almost eighty-year process of adjustment and reform.

Today there is talk of returning more remote communities to Stand Alone Power Systems (SAPS) or microgrids (though there is no consistency in the use of these terms). Proponents of these reforms need to reflect on the history of rural electrification and its relationship to lower prices and higher reliability.

The lessons of the municipal era

That electricity supply initially had public-good characteristics has perpetuated in community expectations. The availability of low-cost electricity is regarded as a social necessity and a requirement for industrial development.

The characteristics of municipal supply were of a very local and 'democratic' approach. Recent interest in Distributed Energy Resources is sometimes associated with a movement to 'democratise' electricity (Ajaz 2019; Burke and Stephens 2017; Thombs 2019; van Veelen and van der Horst

2018). These are social factors not always recognised in economic and engineering studies.

3. State commissions

Two histories detail the developments leading to the creation of state statutory authorities in the five states that later formed the National Electricity Market (NEM) (Allbut 1958; Boehm 1956). State government action became effective in each state in the following years: Tasmania, 1914; Victoria, 1918; New South Wales, 1935; Queensland, 1938; South Australia, 1943; and Western Australia, 1946. Hydro-Tasmania operated as a government department until being converted to a statutory corporation in 1930. The 1935 reform in NSW was only partial until the State Electricity Commission was formed in 1950. The others operated as statutory corporations from these dates.

This move to state authority occurred under governments across the spectrum of Australian political parties.[13]

Progress within the states

Soon after electricity's commercial introduction, state governments legislated to empower various authorities (often municipalities) to generate and supply electricity but otherwise did not play an active role. Tasmania was the first state government to act, setting up the Hydro-Electric Department in 1914 to develop the state's water power resources and supply electricity in bulk to several municipalities and industries, thereby assisting especially the establishment of the metallurgical industry. In 1930, the Hydro-Electric Commission was constituted to take over the development of power resources, and it gradually acquired each local authority's distribution system. It did develop a single fully integrated utility for the entire state.

In Victoria, a statutory corporation, called the State Electricity Commissioners, was constituted in 1918 to initiate the coordinated development of the state's power resources. Victoria had suffered from highly unreliable black coal supplies from NSW and the Victorian Government sought to exploit

---

13   The respective governments at these dates were: Tasmania – Earle (*Labor*); Victoria – Lawson (*Nationalist* or *Liberal*); New South Wales – Stevens and Bruxner (*Liberal* and *Country*); Queensland – Forgan Smith (*Labor*); South Australia – Playford (*Liberal* and *Country*); and Western Australia – Wise (*Labor*). Soon after electricity was introduced commercially, state governments had legislated to empower various authorities (often municipalities) to generate and supply electricity, but otherwise had not played an active role.

its own brown coal resources using techniques developed in Germany. The Victorian development involved building new coal-fired power stations at the site of the coalfields and the investment in high voltage transmission lines as the only practical solution. The need for the coordinated investment in new mines, new power stations and new transmission effectively determined the need for government control.

In his Presidential Address to the 1924 meeting of the Australasian Association for the Advancement of Science, Sir John Monash, first Chairman of the Commission, demonstrated the need for a significant expansion in generating capacity, noting:

> The conclusion is obvious that the immediate attention of Scientists, Engineers and Statesmen is required to satisfying the demand for electrical services which is confronting Australia; that we must evolve far-reaching plans for meeting the situation; and that we must take exhaustive stock of our various resources for power production and estimate their respective extent and capacity and distribution. (Monash 1924)

He noted that the linking up of power stations had already proceeded on a considerable scale in the USA and that Victoria had achieved something in the same direction on a modest scale.

The following developments, according to both Boehm (1956) and Thomis (1987), were influenced by the report *Power Development in Australia* (Gibson 1929).[14] The report noted that 'modern economic development is becoming increasingly dependent upon the supply of power to operate countless machines which mankind has developed for every conceivable purpose' and that all nations 'are straining their efforts to increase the availability and reduce the cost of power supply'. It also observed Australia had a few great cities near the seaboard, country towns and rural centres that were comparatively stagnant, and thus an unbalanced distribution of the population more noticeable than most other countries. Rural power development was thus seen as an economic necessity, citing the earlier development of ports and railways as influences in unleashing the potential of primary production.

---

14   Though this was a Commonwealth Parliamentary Paper tabled in the Senate on 14 August and the House of Representatives on 22 August in 1929, no reference has been found to it in Hansard in the remainder of 1929 or 1930. When the report was tabled, the parliament was already consumed in debating the industrial relations reforms that brought down the Bruce government as the Great Depression began to take hold. It is unsurprising therefore that the report did not feature in debate.

In reaching these conclusions, Gibson referred to two works by his business partner and subsequent first chair of the CSIR (later CSIRO), George Julius. In these papers, Julius made the case that developing Australian manufacturing required greater utilisation of electricity. He argued that the import tariffs on electrical equipment, an industry that was unlikely to be developed in Australia, were holding back the development of electricity supply and use (Julius 1926, 1927).

Gibson's strongest conclusion was that, except for Victoria and Tasmania, the 'organisation for investigating, coordinating, and controlling the supply and distribution of power, is either lacking or insufficient' in the states. Accordingly, he recommended each state constitute an authoritative Power Commission or Power Board. He also recommended that the Commonwealth Government set up a 'suitable organisation' to control national waterways, control electrical energy where it is transferred from one state to another, and ensure the standardisation and coordination of frequency, voltage and methods throughout Australia. Additionally, he proposed that the Commonwealth should assist states 'in every way possible' to develop their power resources. Finally, Gibson suggested that the Chairmen of the State Electricity authorities should meet together under a chairman appointed by the Commonwealth.

While nothing seemed to happen nationally, the report triggered debate in Queensland; then a new Act and Electricity Board in 1933 and eventually a Royal Commission in 1936. The Royal Commission distinguished between state ownership and control. While recognising the state ownership of electricity and other public utilities as 'a contemporary trend or tendency', the Commission recommended creating a State Electricity Commission that would only exercise control. Its first focus was to be south-east Queensland while it would plan for the whole of the state, approving future extensions in the longer term. The Commission commenced in 1938.

The next development was in South Australia, which had no fuel resources and had one major electricity undertaking, the Adelaide Electric Supply Company Ltd. Writing of the company's assistance in wartime, Linn (1996) notes that 'though the company's efforts were laudable, public and parliamentary disquiet about its attitudes bubbled beneath the surface'. Linn gives two fundamental reasons for change: a strong difference of opinion about the regulation of the company between Premier Thomas Playford and the company, and the question of mining and development of brown coal from Leigh Creek.

Playford established an Electricity Supply Committee in March 1943. The Committee favoured Leigh Creek development and recommended the formation of a central supply and generation authority. The South Australian Electricity Commission was established later in 1943. The Commission provided Playford with experts who could assist his cause but only further antagonised the company. In 1944 Playford introduced a Bill to regulate the company's operations further and to limit electricity prices.

The company sought the inclusion in the Bill for a Royal Commission to assess the company's affairs. The Bill then had three parts: the first was to allow trading in the company's shares, the second set an upper limit of 7% on dividends, and the third provided the company with 'the right to a Royal Commission into its affairs' if it felt it had been dealt with unfairly. However, having passed the lower house, the upper house amended the Bill to remove everything other than the calling of a Royal Commission.

The Royal Commission recommended that the Adelaide Electric Supply Company Ltd be acquired by the government and vested in a public utility trust to be set up for the purpose. At the second attempt, Playford had legislation passed in 1946. The company unsuccessfully tried to have the Act challenged in the Privy Council, and the Electricity Trust of South Australia came into existence on 1 September 1946.

In New South Wales, Gibson's criticism of inconsistent standards and inadequate state control led to the passage of the *Gas and Electricity Act 1935*. This Act provided for an Electricity Advisory Committee to which electricity supply authorities were required to submit their development plans (it also included the constitution of the Sydney County Council). The Committee could veto but not amend proposals.

The Second World War was instrumental in increasing electricity demand and a desire for greater security of power supplies which (as noted above) prompted interconnection of the major power stations. This development weakened the opposition of the Local Government Association to the reorganisation of the industry.

Relying on three reports it had received by 1945, the NSW Government strengthened its control by constituting the Electricity Authority of New South Wales in 1945.[15] This was rapidly followed by the establishment of the Electricity Commission of New South Wales in 1950.

---

15   The first report was that of London consulting engineers: Rendel, Palmer and Tritton, *Report on Electrical Development in New South Wales* (Rendel et al. 1937) which recommended the reorganisation of the state into four interconnected systems and the development of a hydro-electric scheme

Its function was to generate and transmit the electricity requirements of the interconnected system to provide bulk power supply to various distribution authorities. The process of acquiring existing generators, building new generators and transmission, and reorganising distribution authorities was ongoing.

Western Australia followed a similar trajectory to other states, though its interconnected system was restricted to the southwest corner. However, as it and the Northern Territory are not formally part of the NEM, their history will not be dealt with in detail. Similarly, the Australian Capital Territory supply is not taken up in this history.

Motivations for reform

The municipal supply system had an interesting mixture of business models across Australia, ranging from municipal-owned undertakings to franchises for private sector supply and cases of municipal undertakings purchasing bulk power supply from other sources. The move to state Commissions mainly eliminated the private ownership model, though it never appears to have been the dominant motivation.

Boehm (1956) proposes five economic and technical forces that promoted the evolution of large-scale central planning of the ESI:

- Savings in capital expenditure on large generating plant, and the savings have been higher than the additional transmission costs involved;
- The pooling of generating capacity provides a significant saving with respect to total capacity;

---

on the Snowy River to add to supply for Sydney. The second report, *Report on the Re-organisation of Electricity Supply in New South Wales*, presented to the state government in 1944, was by Cochran who was the Chair of the State Electricity Commission of Queensland. His report recommended the creation of a Central Electric Authority to be responsible for all electricity development in the state. The third was the *Recommendations of the Electricity Advisory Committee on the Question of the Co-ordination and Control of Electricity Generation and Distribution* (Committee 1945) which was printed as a Parliamentary Paper of New South Wales for 1945–46 along with a report by Premier McKell (1945), *Electricity Co-ordination in Great Britain and Rural Electrification in the United States of America, Great Britain and Canada*. The Committee's recommendations, which Boehm reports as being 'largely endorsed' in the *Electricity Development Act 1945*, are prefaced with the observation 'The Committee re-affirmed its previous recommendations' that a State Electricity Committee should be formed.

- The diversity of loads served by a central authority to a wide area results in a higher load factor of 50–55% compared to 30% for the small local supplier;[16]
- A central authority can view the power requirements of a whole state; and
- Through economies of scale, financial backing, and the use of 'modern techniques', a major authority can exploit resources more quickly and efficiently than small local independent enterprises.

To this should be added government policy for economic development, including metallurgical industries, manufacturing or primary production (and hence rural electrification). Boehm outlines the 'public interest' in electricity supply, quoting from a 1943 South Australian Committee of Inquiry, a concept that sounds much like the current National Electricity Objective:

> The ambit of the term ..., public interest, in its relation to the supply of electricity, requires:
>
> (A) Security – In the form of reliability, continuity, and sufficiency of supply; and
>
> (B) Economy – In the form of the cheapest supply to consumers.

He argues that it would be hard for a private undertaking to justify investment in the public interest that would not provide an adequate return in a short time. Finally, he notes two institutional factors: the exemption of public authorities from income tax and the lower interest rate at which public authorities can raise capital.

As we saw from the complexion of governments that undertook centralisation in each state, the development of the State Electricity model had little to do with ideology. It was instead motivated by practical issues, notably the security of supply and scale efficiency.[17]

In his conclusion, Boehm speculated on the role of the Commonwealth Government and possible future developments. Noting that the advent of the Snowy hydroelectric resources in July 1949 brought the Commonwealth into the field, he suggests that interconnections between the eastern mainland

---

16   Load factor is defined as the average load divided by the peak load **in** a specified time period.

17   This is not the only possible reading of the historic events. For example, Fathollahzadeh (2005) breaks the development of the ESI into five stages and gives it a political economy framework.

states could trigger Commonwealth interest. He adds that another important factor could be the development of atomic energy. He, prophetically, concludes:

> It appears that the Commonwealth has no constitutional authority to participate directly in the development of any State's power resources, apart of course from the Commonwealth's unquestioned authority for defence purposes. It is understandable that in its Constitution no specific reference is made to the development of Australia's electric power resources, although one could infer that, had this matter been considered at the time of Federation, no general authority to undertake electric power except for defence purposes would have been granted to the Commonwealth. Nevertheless, it is possible that should events occur as envisioned above [i.e. interconnections], a central authority could be constituted, of representatives of the Commonwealth and the participant States, to coordinate and to control their development of electric and nuclear power generation and transmission to individual State distribution authorities, in order to satisfy adequately and on the soundest economic basis their various electricity requirements.[18]

Lessons from the development of state commissions

The states developed electricity commissions at very different times across the nation. There were two primary motivating factors. The first was ensuring the security of supply; this was especially the case in Victoria and South Australia, and to a degree in New South Wales. The second was investing for state economic development (this was the motivation in Tasmania and a large part of the motivation in New South Wales and Queensland).

---

18   The constitutional question is indeed interesting. The other major use of electricity – the telegraph and telephone – is a Commonwealth power, though its inclusion is because these services and the post had an international dimension to them. The *Post and Telegraph Bill 1901* as introduced included a clause 136: 'An electric authority shall not construct any electric line or do any other work for the generation use or supply of electricity whereby any telegraph line of the Postmaster-General is or may be injuriously affected.' Debate in the House of Representatives on 28 August 1901 saw contributions from many speakers. W.M. Hughes observed, 'The purport of this clause apparently is to place the whole control of the use of electricity in the hands of the Postmaster-General.' Alfred Deakin observed, 'Our power in regard to electricity is very limited.' William Know and Dugald Thomson between them suggested that the question of electricity regulation might be the subject of 'one of the many conferences which will have to be brought about before the machinery of the States and the Commonwealth will work well together'.

The second lesson is that there were calls for a national approach from the very start of the Commission model, most notably in Monash's Presidential Address and Gibson's report to the Commonwealth Parliament. Writing in 1956, Boehm foreshadowed that the formation of a central authority could follow from the interconnection of state grids. He suggested it could be constituted, of representatives of the Commonwealth and the participant states, to coordinate and control the development of electric power generation and transmission to individual state distribution authorities.

4.   National reform

The road to micro-economic reform

The circumstances considered by Boehm were realised in 1980. The Commonwealth and the governments of New South Wales, Victoria, South Australia and Tasmania appointed a committee to inquire into electricity generation and the sharing of power resources in south-east Australia. Sir David Zeidler chaired the committee, which was made up of representatives from each state electricity body and Snowy Hydro.

The committee's report (Zeidler 1981) first dealt with the prospect of nuclear power based on a study by the State Electricity Commission of Victoria. This study found nuclear power was not cost-competitive with a coal-fired station in New South Wales or Victoria.

In addition, the committee found that high-capacity interconnections could be accomplished using existing technology. However, having examined the overall cost and technical feasibility of further interconnections of the south-east Australian electricity systems, the committee found no justification for doing so within the decade. Nevertheless, the committee recommended that the matter continue to be reviewed as circumstances changed. The committee recommended a limited extension of the NSW–Victoria interconnection to South Australia and that no action be taken on an interconnector to Tasmania.[19]

In 1983, the National Energy Advisory Committee (NEAC) published *Electricity in the Australian Energy Market* (Committee 1983) (its nineteenth report). Minister for Natural Resources Doug Anthony established the NEAC in 1977. Its role was to 'advise the government on energy matters and assist

---

19   Booth (2000), who is generally critical of the market reform program, argues that the Zeidler committee was intentionally misled by state power companies.

in the formulation and development of a national energy policy in Australia' (Anthony 1977). Before it ceased to exist in 1983, the NEAC produced twenty-one reports, covering a diverse range of energy topics, including energy conservation, electric vehicles and renewable energy resources.

The report found that the share of electricity in final energy demand (consumption) had grown from 11% in 1970–71 to 14% in 1980–81. The share of natural gas had grown faster from 3% to 13%. It observed that oil displacement by electricity and gas was consistent with an energy policy to reduce dependence on oil.

An additional finding was that the level of electricity prices began to rise in real terms at the end of the 1970s, having declined for over twenty years before that. Figure 1 provides a chart of real residential and non-residential electricity prices from 1955 to 2020 using aggregate consumption and revenue data where available and the ABS CPI index otherwise. The chart clearly shows the initial ending of the price declines in the late 1970s.

Figure 1:
Historic residential and non-residential real per kWh electricity prices

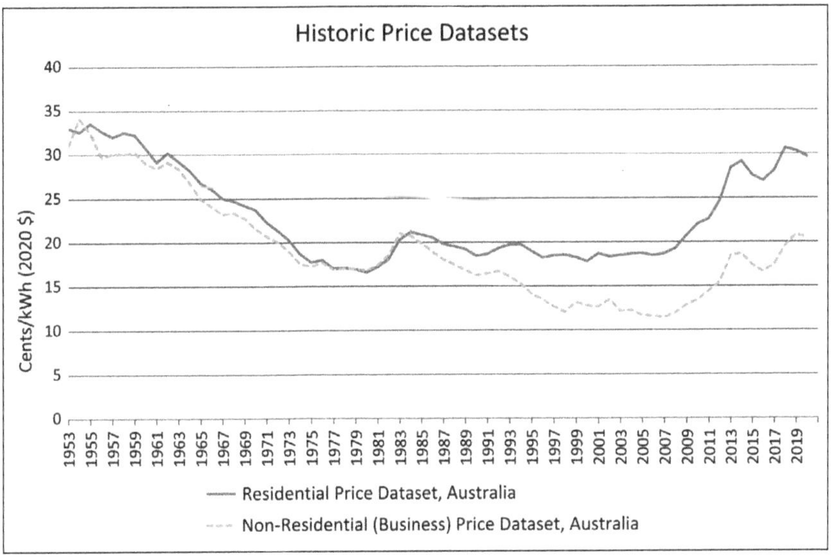

Source: Havyatt 2021.

However, the report's major conclusion was that 'the efficient and economic development of the electricity supply industry in the future will, as in the past, depend to a significant degree on the extent to which appropriate pricing policies are followed'.

So, not for the last time, a recommendation from a review was to accelerate the reform of tariffs. This recommendation included both the use of time of use or demand tariffs and the possibility of 'concessional tariffs for a lower reliability supply' to reduce the need for plant reserve margins. It also recommended the consideration of broad targets for improvements in operating efficiency. However, no evidence has been found of any action on these recommendations.

The next significant development was what can only be called the disaster that befell the State Electricity Commission of Victoria.

Evans (2004) provides a positive view of changes in the early 1980s. He asserts that 'the typical electricity organisation up to the 1970s was bureaucratic and mechanistic in form and structure ... electricity planning was positivistic'. However, the success of large plants realising economies of scale resulted in the electricity supply industry being surprised by the levelling of demand in the late 1970s. As a consequence of 'the embedded engineering pro-development culture' of such organisations and the levelling of demand, Evans reports that 'by the mid-1980s, planned expansions to existing excess generating capacity in New South Wales, Queensland and Victoria were cause for serious concern'. He concludes his piece with a rollicking tale of progressive improvement in management and culture at the State Electricity Commission of Victoria (SECV). He tracks this as a change from managerialism introduced under the incoming ALP government in 1982 through commercialisation, corporatisation and privatisation.

Booth (2000) tells a different tale of the quality of management in the ESI, summarised in his description of Australia as 'not so much a nation, but more a series of warring tribes'. He recounts first the many problems that the SECV had with developing the Yallourn and Hazelwood power stations before settling in on the 'Newport saga'. Because of the continuing poor performance of the Latrobe Valley power stations and because oil was plentiful and cheap, in the late 1960s the SECV planned a 200MW peaking plant to the west of Melbourne, at either Werribee or Geelong near the oil refinery. However, the engineers took over the project and 'became preoccupied with continuing to utilise the Newport power station site'. The project morphed away from a small peaking plant well away from the city to become two large 500MW units in the city that offended its neighbours, the unions and environmentalists. It was converted to gas after the Bass Strait discoveries that were made available to Melbourne in 1969. Thankfully, Victorians were saved from using oil at Newport when the oil price shock came in the middle of the 1970s.

The disasters of the Loy Yang project dwarfed Newport's problems. When given parliamentary approval in 1976, the project would match world's best practice in brown coal plants. It was mainly the cost estimates for Loy Yang, that the total cost of energy from brown coal would match that from black coal, that meant the SECV was able to convince Zeidler against the need for further interconnections.

Following the election of the ALP in Victoria, the SECV had to confess to a significant 65–70% blow-out in costs and the doubling of forecast operating costs. However, with some management changes and in response to targets set by the Labor government, Loy Yang was brought online in 1986 in line with earlier budgets and operating with an availability of 81%, well above the other La Trobe plants.[20] The huge disaster was the development of Loy Yang B 1&2. Projected to cost $1700 million, but ultimately delivered at $2800 million, it led to the near-bankruptcy of the SECV.

It was later revealed that NSW had offered to complete the Mt Piper project, construction of which had ceased due to lack of demand, at the cost of $320 million and to augment the necessary transmission. In late 1986 the Victorian Government initiated an inquiry by the National Resources and Environment Committee (NREC) of the Victorian Parliament. It concluded that, unlike the Zeidler conclusions in 1980, the cost of power from Victorian brown coal plants had risen to 50% more than buying power from black coal plants in the northern states.

The states and their Electricity Commissions were not alone in their folly. In the late 1970s and early 1980s, Australia experienced its fourth resources boom (Battellino 2010). In his policy speech for the 1980 election campaign, Prime Minister Malcolm Fraser referred to the $6000 million investment in mining and manufacturing that had occurred since he forecast it would in his 1977 policy speech. He forecast further investment of $29,000 million (Fraser 1980). Concerning electricity, he said:

> Let me give you another measure of what is happening in Australia. The increase in electricity generation through the 1980s will be almost equal to that which occurred over the last 30 years. We are going to do in ten years what previous generations took 30 years to accomplish.

---

20   It is instructive that the initial Loy Yang problems occurred before the ALP won office, and it was the Labor government's intervention that got it on track. Subsequent SECV disasters were on Labor's watch, but the issue seems to have been the organisation not the government. Booth is also highly critical of the Victorian choice of 500kV transmission lines.

Fraser manifested his support for expansion in electricity generation with special dispensations from the Loans Council for infrastructure investment (Kellow 1996).[21] However, the 1980s are not the last time there has been an overestimation of future demand.

Micro-economic reform

Borland (2015) claimed that the idea that micro-economic reform 'constituted a broad and coherent episode of policymaking' had only gradually become apparent. He notes that 'The story of government intervention in the Australian economy in the 30 years after World War 2 has been described as "All the restrictive practices known to man".'

It is, without doubt, a significant simplification to describe economic policy post-1945 as consisting of two periods, Keynesian and neoliberal. Cornish (1993) is critical of the thesis of a 'Keynesian revolution in economic policy commencing in the 1940s' as Australian governments had always been interventionist. However, there was a very decided change in approach starting in the mid-1980s. For example, the reforms to the electricity supply industry were labelled as part of a 'micro-economic reform agenda' by Prime Minister Hawke in a February 1990 campaign speech (Hawke 1990b).

McLean (2013) notes that the micro-economic reforms of the 1980s and 90s had their origins in reforms in the 1970s, while the Industry Commission noted that 'Interest in the gains from microeconomic reform dates back at least to the report of the Vernon Committee in the mid-1960s' (Industry Commission 1995).

The Industries Assistance Commission (IAC), a replacement of the Tariff Board, was moved to the Treasury portfolio in 1988 (Productivity Commission 2003).[22] The Treasurer announced a substantial forward work program for the IAC, saying:

---

21   It is sometimes described that Fraser lost office because the resources boom never came to pass (see, for example, Alex Millmow, 'Malcolm Fraser's life and legacy: Experts respond', The Conversation 20 March 2015, https://theconversation. com/malcolm-frasers-life-and-legacy-experts-respond-39111). The issue was that the boom existed but failed to continue. A source of the boom had been investment in energy resources to substitute for oil after the oil shock, but the shock otherwise caused a global slowdown.

22   The Industries Assistance Commission was the second incarnation of a function called the Tariff Board, and was replaced by the Industries Commission and ultimately the Productivity Commission (Productivity Commission 2003).

The sharp deterioration of Australia's terms of trade over the past two years, and the more recent troubles in world share markets, have highlighted the need for our industries to become and remain internationally competitive, for efficiency to be improved across-the-board and for impediments to change to be removed.

... While the Commission will continue to conduct inquiries of a traditional kind into particular industries, the Government now intends that it also conduct broader ranging inquiries directed towards removing impediments to improved efficiency across the whole spectrum of industry. (Treasurer, Press release, no. 7, 26 January 1988, quoted in Industry Commission 1995, p. 53)

An inquiry into government (non-tax) charges was one of four included in a forward work program on this agenda, and a report on the electricity supply industry in Australia was released on 17 March 1989 (IAC 1989). The report found excessive generation capacity, tariffs discriminating in favour of rural users and domestic customers, and revenue not recovering actual costs. The 'true costs' not being recovered included an allowance for a market-based cost of capital rather than the simple recovery of historic costs plus any loan terms from governments. The report also found that the internal operating environment of the electricity utilities under government ownership compared unfavourably to the private sector as management was faced with conflicting objectives, government interference, and pricing policies established to promote social and regional development outcomes.

The Commission noted reforms already underway but further noted that 'the benefits from such reforms could be increased if interconnections between the states were strengthened. Interconnections would enhance the potential for trade in electricity across state borders. The Commission estimated this reform to have potential benefits of about $180 million annually.'

It is easy to overestimate the significance of the IAC's report. As McDonell (1989) notes:

When the National Resources and Environment Committee of the Victorian Parliament reported in April last on its enquiry into electricity supply beyond the mid-1990s, its themes were similar to some of those of the NSW Inquiry into Electricity Generation Planning whose report was tabled 12 months previously – uncertainty in demand growth, planning flexibility, better plant performance, greater inter-State coordination, alternative energy sources, demand management, conservation.[23]

McDonell notes that the overhang of supply built into the accelerated power station development programs in the 1970s and 1980s, together with the fall-off in demand, created significant problems and opportunities for reform. He goes on to state, 'For social, economic and operational reasons the role of inter-State planning and coordination is very important and should be greatly strengthened. Much of the overhang is the result of the past lack of development coordination between the two major States and joint planning would reduce future capital and resource requirement.' He states:

> This paper canvasses some of the implications of the interconnection of the four systems, the introduction of gas as a fuel for power generation, the development of national energy markets and their operating and regulatory structures, and opportunities for national coordination in providing better conditions for pricing and investment.[24]

Fulfilling the election commitment on micro-economic reform, the Commonwealth convened a Special Premiers Conference in October 1990. In his opening statement, the Prime Minister said, 'our agreed goal can be simply stated ... to make the Federation work better' (Hawke 1990a). He continued:

> An important objective for this first special Conference is to reach broad agreement on a set of principles, as a clear guide for future action in the key areas under review. Those areas which we are looking at today cover the full range of inter-governmental relationships: the general financial relationships; tied grants; micro-economic reform; duplication of services; the environment; and industrial relations.

The Communique extracted from the records of the conference on electricity generation, transmission and distribution reads, under the heading of 'micro-economic reform':

> Leaders agreed that there may be additional benefits from an extension of, and/or organisational changes to, the interstate electricity network

---

23   The cited reports have not been read for this review.
24   This paragraph makes for powerful reading thirty years later as we grapple with proposals to significantly augment the interconnections and as the Commonwealth Government has backed greater utilisation of gas as a transition fuel.

covering NSW, Victoria, Queensland, South Australia, Tasmania and the ACT. Consequently, they further agreed that a working group be set up to:

(a) assess whether extensions to the interstate network are economically justified;

(b) if so, assess the organisational options for achieving this, including a jointly owned interstate transmission system, a pool arrangement, and other ways of improving the management of current interstate arrangements; and

(c) report to the next Special Premiers' Conference.

The working group will include representation from relevant electricity authorities and policy agencies from the respective governments including the Commonwealth, and seek contributions from interested parties, including major users in the private sector.

In the light of Australian debates over the last decade, it is interesting to note that the Communique, under the heading of the environment, records:

On the greenhouse effect, Leaders noted that the Commonwealth and States were already implementing a policy of phasing out chloro-fluorocarbons and halons by 1997, in advance of the Montreal Protocol. State and Territory governments endorsed the Commonwealth's decision to adopt an interim planning target of stabilising emissions of green-house gases not controlled by the Montreal Protocol, based on 1988 levels, by the year 2000, and reducing these emissions by 20 per cent by the year 2005.

The Commonwealth and the States agreed that both levels of government would co-operate on a national greenhouse strategy. This strategy would include measures for limiting emissions of all greenhouse gases and adapting to climate change, for conducting further research and ensuring that the community understood the need for early action and the measures individuals could take ...

The States strongly supported Australian efforts to get an international convention on climate change, and they agreed with the Commonwealth that Australia should not implement response measures that would have net adverse economic impacts nationally or on Australia's trade competitiveness, in the absence of similar action by major greenhouse gas producing countries.

They also recognised, however, that new economic and trade opportunities could open up for Australia through the development of more environmentally sound processes and products, and all governments agreed to encourage industry to take up this challenge vigorously.

In May, two months after the 1990 election and just fourteen months after receiving the IAC's report, the Treasurer tasked the now renamed Industries Commission with another inquiry on gas and electricity. The terms of reference called for a report on 'institutional, regulatory or other arrangements subject to influence by government in Australia which lead to inefficient resource use, and advice on courses of action to reduce or remove such inefficiencies'.

Among the list of items to which the Commission should prioritise were the scope for rationalisation by interconnection, the appropriateness of various load management and energy conservation initiatives to enhance efficiency and the relative efficiency and cost-effectiveness of options to reduce the environmental impact of burning fossil fuels. The last of these was removed from the terms of reference in December 1990 when the Treasurer gave the Commission a separate reference on greenhouse gases emissions. (That report appeared in 1991; IC 1991.)

The Industry Commission delivered the Report in May 1991. It advanced the following proposals concerning the ESI:

- All public electricity and gas utilities to be corporatised as soon as possible, preferably within twelve months.
- The separation of generation and transmission, introduced in two stages – the first through ring-fencing for up to two years before complete separation.
- The creation of power pooling arrangements through 'various markets' (the IAC report had previously noted that the state Commissions were already using merit order administrative arrangements).
- The various generating activities of the state Commissions to be broken up to give a spur to competition.
- The distribution function (where not already so) to be separated from transmission (distribution was separate in NSW and Queensland and in the case of eleven municipal undertakings handling 20% of the electricity in Victoria). This should also be introduced in two stages.

- That distribution be operated through several separate authorities, each large enough to provide economies of scale but providing enough entities to use 'yardstick' regulation.
- The integration of a national grid entity that would be accountable to a Council of Ministers, with independent regulatory oversight. The development of the new arrangements to be the responsibility of a Steering Committee comprising representatives of participating governments rather than utilities. (Note the state Commissions favoured a model of the existing arrangements coordinated by a National Grid Management Council.)
- The activities of the national grid, distribution authorities and other entities to be subject only to the general monitoring provisions of the Trade Practices Commission and the Prices Surveillance Authority.
- With the possible exception of the transmission segment, nothing about the ESI justified continuing public ownership. Instead, the Commission recommended governments sell their generating assets and progressively sell their distribution assets.
- Governments address the institutional impediments (e.g. government policies which prevent energy prices from reflecting supply costs) and market failures (e.g. environmental concerns and information gaps) that impede the efficient use of energy, provided it can be demonstrated that net benefits would result.

All the elements of the reform program, including separation, are included here – two years before the Competition Policy Review by Hilmer.

The Special Premiers Conference that followed, however, did not fully execute the Industry Commission Plan. Nevertheless, the Communique notes that leaders agreed to establish a National Grid Management Council (NGMC). The NGMC's function was 'to encourage and coordinate the most efficient, economic and environmentally sound development of the electricity industry in eastern and southern Australia having regard for key National and State policy objectives'. It noted, 'This represents an important step forward in advancing co-operation in the electricity industry, the absence of which has cost the nation dearly in terms of excessive generation capacity, inappropriate plant mix and inflexibility of fuel use.'

Each participating government was to nominate a representative to the Council, which was to have an independent chairperson. The Council's task was to oversee the preparation of a draft protocol to be presented to Heads of Government for consideration in November 'covering the planning, operation, development, monitoring and extension of the eastern and southern Australia grid'.

The Communique notes that leaders agreed that extensions to the current interstate grid were technically feasible and economically justified. With an expectation of further details being prepared for the November meeting, it was noted a link to Tasmania could be operational by the mid to late 1990s and the extension to Queensland possibly from 1997.

From NGMC to AEMO

The Commonwealth Government learned quickly that the supply authorities did not share the Premiers' commitment to these reforms. The single biggest difference between the two (IAC and IC) reports and the work being undertaken by the states was the emphasis in the Commonwealth reports on interconnection.

The agreement between the states for establishing the NGMC appeared to be quite clear in its definition of the National Grid:

> The Council will define the South and East Australian National Grid ('the Grid') in terms of the elements of the transmission networks of the State and Territory-owned electricity utilities of the participating States and Territories, and any privately owned or other elements, that comprise the Grid. (National Archives of Australia: Department of Prime Minister and Cabinet; A1209 1991)

However, the Commonwealth Government soon realised that the process would not run smoothly. Less than a year later, in a briefing note to Prime Minister Paul Keating before the next leaders meeting, Rod Sims (then a Deputy Secretary in the Department of Prime Minister and Cabinet) noted that the generally agreed approach to reform was via internal restructuring and the introduction of competition. However, he raised doubt about whether the National Grid Management Council could achieve its aims. He said the NGMC was 'a cooperative venture in an industry accustomed to barriers to entry and the monopoly rents associated with them' (National Archives of Australia: Department of Prime Minister and Cabinet; A1209 1992a).

In talking points for discussion with Premiers Greiner and Kirner, Sims suggests that if these discussions do not contain a commitment to enter into agreements to establish a National Grid Corporation, the PM should 'urge them at the next conference to agree to "work towards an NGC"', subject to settling some issues. The memo also notes that initial pool arrangements had been operating in NSW since 1 January 1992 and that Pacific Power (the renamed Electricity Commission) would be introducing its electricity exchange market (ELEX) from 1 July 1992. He noted that Victorian reform was pursuing a substantially different approach with long-term contracting and retention of distribution within SECV.

Commenting on the meeting in a press conference (Keating 1992), Prime Minister Keating observed:

> Moving now to electricity generation, which was another 'One Nation' topic we had on the agenda, we did secure agreement in principle to the separation of power generation from transmission. This is the key point in this issue – that the providers of power are not the transmitters of power with a view to establishing an East-Coast electricity grid, a network which would be represented by a structure yet to be agreed … In other words, that the transmission assets of the East-Coast State would be part of an East-Coast grid, a body, a corporation … but the principle of separation is agreed.

In preparation for the next leaders meeting, Peter Harris drafted a memo on what might need to be achieved (National Archives of Australia: Department of Prime Minister and Cabinet; A1209 1992b). He first noted that state governments had told the NGMC that they did not need the $100 million earmarked in 'One Nation' for transmission augmentation. He further observed that the Business Council of Australia and Australian Mining Industry Council were keen to join the NGMC, which at the time was dominated by electricity generators (although Victoria and NSW claimed to be preparing to replace these with state officials). In considering how to address the membership question, Harris noted:

> We are at a point where if we do not cut the utilities down to size, we will have achieved the equivalent of putting Telecom in charge of the telecommunications reform process (remember that Telecom supported competition in 1990, just that it wanted competition on its own terms).

On the topic of a National Grid Corporation, Harris surmised that the Commonwealth did not have much prospect of getting up a National Grid Corporation, noting the NGMC appeared to be committed to only ring-fencing transmission from generation. He noted that a proposal had been put together to claim that separate multiple network corporations would be set up. However, Harris expressed his view that this wasn't what the Prime

Minister got the leaders to accept at the previous meeting. He further noted that the Chair of the NGMC had warned NSW and SA that their attitude risked destroying the NGMC, adding that 'We believe the NGMC will be publicly criticised (as it is, now, privately by people such as Kerry Schott) as nothing more than a generators club.' He concluded the note by suggesting that 'pressing Premiers to pay some attention to the NGMC' was also not a bad idea. 'While we cannot always expect that State officials will do a better job on pro-competitive issues, they can do no worse than their utilities.'

In a further note to Rod Sims, Harris noted that the Prime Minister's intervention had proven pivotal in getting the NGMC to move beyond ring-fencing. All utilities had 'rolled over' for multiple network corporations that would place state transmission companies under some form of coordinated control. He noted it is a short step from there to the point where the controller (described as the National Electricity Board) takes on responsibility for merit order dispatch and settlement.

He noted that ring fencing would be used as an interim step. He also noted that inevitably a neutral, independently managed grid arrangement would not have been created by July 1993, when the NGMC timetable suggested there was supposed to be a customer market in electricity in operation. Consequently, he suggested that the timing for the commitment to a customer market should be revisited.

This dive into the archives is used to demonstrate the ways incumbents and the states disrupted the reform plans. For example, while ELEX was operating in July 1992, the expansion to a fully functioning NEM only occurred in 1998, and full retail contestability was slowly rolled out from 2002 to 2013.

The new arrangements were formally introduced by the *National Electricity (South Australia) Act 1996*. The market was operated by the National Electricity Market Management Company (NEMMCO) under a code authorised by the ACCC. Obligations of market participants were enforced by the National Electricity Code Administrator (NECA). NEMMCO and NECA were joint ventures of Queensland, New South Wales, the Australian Capital Territory, Victoria, South Australia and Tasmania. Full retail contestability (FRC) with regulated prices commenced in all states other than Queensland and Tasmania between 1 January 2002 and 1 July 2003. Queensland progressed to FRC in 2006 and Tasmania in 2013. Price deregulation occurred from 2008 to 2015 but still does not apply in regional Queensland and Tasmania (AEMC 2017).

In 2001 the Council of Australian Governments (COAG) issued a statement on energy policy *Towards a National Energy Policy* (COAG 2007). After noting the reform progress since the 1991 Industry Commission report, the statement noted, 'there remain immediate and long-term issues that need to be addressed. They include National Electricity Market (NEM) issues of capacity, interconnection, pricing (including transmission pricing), NEM governance, and regulatory overlap, the facilitation of increased market penetration of natural gas and improved demand management.'

It noted agreed objectives of:

- Encouraging the efficient provision of reliable, competitively-priced energy services to Australians, underpinning wealth and job creation and improved quality of life, taking into account the needs of regional, rural and remote areas;
- Encouraging responsible development of Australia's energy resources, technology and expertise, their efficient use by industries and households and their exploitation in export markets; and
- Mitigating local and global environmental impacts, notably green-house impacts, of energy production, transformation, supply and use.

Three areas of priority action supported these objectives:

- National energy policy leadership – the statement announced the establishment of the Ministerial Council on Energy (MCE). The MCE was requested to report back after its first meeting on 'key approaches and handling timetables' for a suite of issues. The issues included likely energy use scenarios over the next decade, the potential for harmonising regulatory arrangements, opportunities to increase interconnection and system security, and ways of accelerating improved consumer choice. The statement suggested that improving consumer choice would involve 'providing better information and enhancing cooperative energy efficiency activities and decision making for demand-side participation'.[25]

---

25 It is an interesting fact that the 'collective of energy ministers' was only formed in 2007. A Council of Ministers had been central to the 1991 Industries Commission proposals. Since 2007 the MCE has been renamed as the Standing Committee on Energy and Resources (SCER) and the COAG Energy Council. Following the Morrison government's abolition of COAG, the collective of energy ministers now officially meets in two guises. The first is as the Energy National Cabinet Reform Committee while the former COAG Energy Council will be replaced by an Energy Ministers' Meeting that will focus on priorities that are not covered by the Energy National Cabinet Reform Committee (see http://www.coagenergycouncil.gov.au/news/new-energy-ministers-meeting).

- Immediate action on high-priority National Electricity Market issues – the statement tasked the recently formed NEM Ministers Forum with giving urgent attention to several NEM issues. These included impediments to investment in interconnection, transmission pricing, regulatory overlap, market behaviour (e.g. re-bidding), and the effectiveness of regulatory arrangements in promoting efficient market outcomes. The Forum was also asked to address regional boundaries and demand-side participation.
- The statement announced that there would be a high-level independent strategic review of medium- to longer-term energy market directions. The terms of reference for the review included identifying impediments to the realisation of the benefits of energy market reform and strategic directions for further reform. It specifically sought advice on 'regulatory approaches that effectively balance incentives for new supply investment, demand responses and benefits to consumers' and 'assessing the relative efficiency and cost-effectiveness of options within the energy market to reduce greenhouse gas emissions from the electricity and gas sectors'.

The review report, *Towards a Truly National and Efficient Energy Market* (Parer 2002), detailed what it called 'serious energy market deficiencies', listing:

- The energy sector governance arrangements are confused; there is excessive regulation and perceptions of conflict of interest.
- There is insufficient generator competition to allow Australia's gross pool system to work as intended.
- Electricity transmission investment and operation are flawed, and the current regions do not reflect the market's needs.
- The financial contracts market is extremely illiquid, in part reflecting considerable regulatory uncertainty.
- There are many impediments to the demand side playing its true role in the market.
- There is insufficient competition in the east coast gas market and too much uncertainty surrounding new pipeline development.
- Greenhouse responses so far are ad hoc and poorly targeted.
- The NEM is currently disadvantaging some regional areas.

It recommended simplifying the governance arrangements by creating a National Energy Regulator to encompass the energy-specific roles of the ACCC, all the state and territory regulatory bodies, and some of the roles of NECA, and for an enhanced role for NEMMCO in terms of proactive market development.

Concerning transmission, it proposed giving NEMMCO responsibility for all transmission planning and that NEMMCO should auction firm transmission rights (FTRs). Furthermore, it proposed that the traded prices for FTRs should trigger investment in further inter-regional transmission. It also proposed increasing the number of regions with 'full nodal pricing as the longer-term goal'.

In relation to demand-side participation issues, the report proposed the mandated rollout of interval meters and the removal of retail price caps. In addition, so that the demand-side could gain total value for the capability it brings, the report proposed a 'pay-as-bid' mechanism into NEMMCO dispatch and settlement.

The report proposed abolishing most existing schemes on greenhouse emissions, including the Commonwealth's Mandatory Renewable Energy Target. Instead, the report recommended an economy-wide emissions trading system replace these schemes.

The MCE response to COAG embraced the recommendations but stopped short of anything that impinged upon state regulation. In responding to the governance recommendations, the MCE proposed the creation of both the Australian Energy Regulator as proposed by Parer but also created the AEMC as a rule maker and body responsible for market development. While agreeing that 'further reform should be undertaken to address *greenhouse emissions* from the energy sector, in the light of concerns about climate change and the need for a stable long-term framework for investment in energy supplies' the MCE only proposed to 'work closely with the COAG High-Level Group on Greenhouse to address greenhouse gas emissions from the energy sector on a national basis'.

The question of economic regulation was handed to another review (Beale et al. 2006), and later the Energy Reform Implementation Group (ERIG) provided its report *Energy Reform: The Way Forward for Australia* (Scales 2007). The terms of reference for the latter was led by a requirement for ERIG to provide reform recommendations for 'achieving a fully national transmission grid including the most suitable governance and transitional arrangements having regard for COAG's objective of achieving a truly national approach to the future development of the electricity grid'.

The Scales report itself was scathing of the governance arrangements for the sector, and that improvement was a 'critical pre-condition for continued improvement'. The report noted that it 'strongly believed' that 'single

Australia-wide, energy market-wide, independent (and preferably separate) institutions covering planning, market operation, market regulation and rule-making are urgently required and would be the logical evolution of current market governance arrangements'. It proposed that sharpening the separation between the role of the MCE as the peak policymaking body and the bodies responsible for planning, operating, rule-making and regulation of Australia's energy markets would improve governance, including ensuring the independence of market operators from governments. Increasing the influence of the Commonwealth or COAG in the oversight and development and monitoring of Australia's energy policy and 'clarifying and strengthening the role of the Commonwealth Government within the MCE would help as well'.

It also found that the AEMC needed reform, noting it needed 'to be adequately and transparently funded, preferably by the Commonwealth Government, and to have more control over its own work programme, subject to being required to develop rules that enhance market efficiency'. It also proposed reforms to NEMMCO, including that a 'national energy market operator should replace the separate operators for gas and electricity'. On the issue of transmission, the report proposed the creation of a new National Transmission Planner function that would be placed within NEMMCO if the appropriate reforms to NEMMCO were made.[26]

The response to both these reports resulted in the creation of AEMO to replace NEMCO and the adoption of consistent definitions of the objective of the national gas and electricity laws.

Current status

Three further significant reviews have 'reported' on the market: the *Review of Governance Arrangements for Australian Energy Markets* (Vertigan et al. 2015), the *Blueprint for the Future: Independent Review into the Future Security of the National Electricity Market* (Finkel 2017) and the *Retail Electricity Pricing Inquiry* (ACCC 2018a). However, action on recommendations has been inconsistent. Almost the only consistency has been the inability of the jurisdictions to agree on any proposals that strengthen the national character of regulation and institutions and a reluctance to empower the market bodies.

---

26 It is somewhat amusing to note that the ERIG report discusses a submission from the Energy Users Association of Australia that 'one option for delivering national co-ordination and the identification of optimal projects to transmission in the NEM would be the establishment of a national grid company'. This is noted without any reference to it being the Commonwealth's initial preferred approach.

The Vertigan review observed that the energy system was undergoing an unprecedented rate of change but that a strategic policy deficit existed. Nothing in the operation of energy ministers' meetings or the operation of the market bodies fundamentally addressed this. The one recommendation for energy ministers to develop a strategic plan with the assistance of the AEMC was soon overtaken by a Finkel recommendation for an Energy Security Board to write such a plan.

Finkel's recommended Energy Security Board (ESB) consisted of a new chair and deputy chair with the heads of the three market bodies. It was created as a coordination mechanism between the market bodies and an entity to steer significant reform. Its first foray into reform, the National Energy Guarantee, attempted to replace disparate climate policies with an effective emissions trading scheme within the electricity market. However, it failed to gain support and ultimately cost Prime Minister Turnbull his position.

The ESB was then engaged in turning a half-thought idea from a meeting of energy ministers in October 2018 into a new market design under the banner of the post-2025 project.

At the creation of the ESB, it was announced that it would be reviewed after three years, and the review report was completed in June 2020 (Edwards & Consulting 2020). In their response to the review (Energy Ministers 2020), energy ministers agreed to extend the term of the ESB to December 2021 'pending completion of the post-2025 market design project' and that they will consider options for future energy governance arrangements in mid-2021. In addition, the response noted 'transition planning for the cessation of the ESB should include a proposal for a Market Bodies Forum (MBF)'. Interestingly the market bodies had launched just such a forum as an attempt to forestall the Finkel recommendation for the ESB (AER 2017).

Following the receipt of the ESB's Post-2025 Market Design recommendations in July 2021, the energy ministers gave effect to their 2020 plan. They restructured the ESB as just the three leaders of the market bodies, to be chaired by the Chair of the AEMC.

Finally, the ACCC's pricing inquiry (REPI) found that in the period 2008 to 2018, multiple factors had caused the sharp increases in retail prices, as shown in Figure 1. High on the list were increased network charges that had two sources. The first was the imposition of higher reliability standards by the NSW and Queensland governments, and the second was another round of overestimating demand. Figure 2 shows the NEM forecast and actual demand from 2004–05. It took the forecasters five years to identify the downturn in demand as a permanent feature caused by greater energy efficiency and rooftop PV, among other factors.

Figure 2: NEM forecast and actual demand 2004–05 to 2022–23

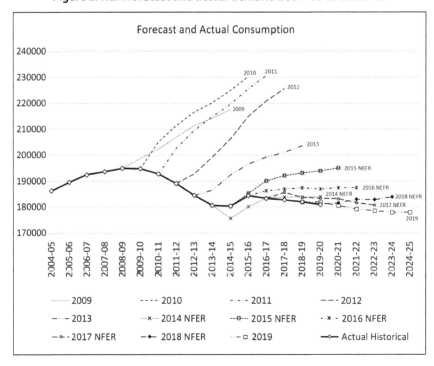

Source: Author's figure based on AEMO data.

Lessons from the move to the NEM and after

The issue of electricity prices became a concern of the federal government in the context of developments exposing more Australian industry to competition from imports. The government's studies found gross inefficiencies in the development of electricity, including an overinvestment in generating capabilities. The IAC report concluded that facilitating interstate trade in electricity would overcome this tendency to overdevelopment.

The implementation of this system faced strong resistance from the electricity commissions, and the preferred model of a National Grid was abandoned. The actual implementation of the NEM took seven years from conception. Despite the Industry Commission's call for a governing body drawn from governments rather than utilities, this was not implemented until 2001.

The further development of a national market has constituted a long series of incremental and not consistently uniform reforms. Moreover, state ministers' concerns about reliability in their jurisdiction have threatened the efficiency of the integrated grid.

5.   Conclusions

Opinions on the progress of energy sector reform cover a broad spectrum. Some support the theme expressed by the title of an AEMC publication, *The National Electricity Market: A Case Study in Successful Microeconomic Reform* (AEMC and KPMG 2013). On the other hand, some may be critical of the outcome but less so of the process, such as:

> Australia's microeconomic policy agenda in the 1990s led to the structural reform of the electricity and gas industries [Hilmer (1993) is then cited for the original competition policy recommendations related to structural separation of public monopolies]. State Electricity Commissions had historically been responsible for operating electricity systems within jurisdictional boundaries … The reform of electricity generation and creation of the NEM could be argued to have been the centrepiece of microeconomic reform of the East-coast electricity market. (Nelson and Orton 2016)

Others take a more radical view, focused mainly on the question of whether markets can deliver an efficient ESI, such as:

> The conclusion must be that the disaggregated, disconnected market is not working sufficiently well to provide reliable electricity at affordable prices and that some further radical reshaping of the market is now needed. (Aulich and Wettenhall 2017)

What is incontrovertible is that the real price of electricity, having been mainly stable for two decades, suddenly and dramatically increased from about 2007 (ACCC 2018b). The divergence happens to coincide with the GFC and the impact of the drought that drove up wholesale prices in 2007–08 through shortage of hydroelectric supply and some generators not having water for cooling (Moran and Sood 2013). But it also coincides with the point at which steady per-household consumption growth reversed and the move to the national economic regulation of networks under highly deficient rules.

Writing in 2008, Moran and Skinner note that 'a key debate surrounding electricity markets remains the general question of resource adequacy. That is, can we leave investment in long-lead time and long-lived assets, producing a product essential to every other part of the economy, to the chaos of a free market?' (Moran and Skinner 2008). They conclude that the NEM had been successful, particularly because the bias of electricity commissions to 'base load' stations had been replaced by more investment in peaking generators. Further, the peaking generators responded to the opportunities in the market and improved their operations to be able to generate within two hours rather than the five that had previously been their performance.

This review has listed only some of the many Royal Commissions, inquiries, expert reviews and legislative reforms over the 132 years since the use of electricity to light Tamworth's streets. As policy makers and market bodies confront the challenges that accompany the transition of energy systems to a zero-carbon future, there are two conclusions from this history that need to be kept in mind.

The first is that the dominant narrative of a relatively stable ESI operated through vertically integrated state-owned entities until reformed in response to Hilmer's competition policy is false. The reality is different:

- The ESI began as a complex mix of public and private municipal-scale enterprises.
- The move to create State Electricity Commissions (or equivalent) happened at very different times and under different motivations in each state.
- Heading into the 1990s, only the ACT, South Australia and Tasmania supplied electricity entirely through the vertical operation of the state Commission – in Victoria, 20% of distribution continued through municipal enterprises, while in NSW and Queensland all distribution was beyond the control of the Commission.
- The reform process was triggered more by the interest in interstate trade in energy as a means to reduce electricity prices to industry than by general competition policy, and it was triggered before the creation of the Hilmer committee.
- There has been a continual change process, but the pace has always been much slower than those who instigate change envision.

The second conclusion is that the same issues have been recycling for thirty years, including:

- Despite the motivation for the NEM being an oversupply of generation, policy makers' most significant concern has always been resource adequacy (of both generation and transmission).
- The desire for demand management and demand-side participation has been a constant unrealised goal.
- The need to reduce greenhouse gas emissions has been an ever-present goal without effective action.

- The self-interest of energy companies and jurisdictional officials has dominated policy outcomes.

Hugh Outhred, credited in the Acknowledgements of the seminal *Spot Pricing of Electricity* (Schweppe et al. 1988), observed in the introduction and conclusion of a conference paper extolling the success of the Australian reforms of the 1990s:

> Electricity restructuring is a complex, never-ending process that has engineering, economic, commercial, legal and policy dimensions and takes place within a broad societal context that itself influences and is influenced by the outcome … Success depends on establishing and maintaining a consensus on the key objectives and principles … The dynamic and evolving nature of the broader social context means that there can be no guarantee of future stability and continuity in approach to electricity industry restructuring. For example [the AEMC's *Comprehensive Reliability Review*] opens up the possibility of a complete re-think of the current approach to addressing the perennial and irresolvable (in a deterministic sense) question of 'resource adequacy'.

History shows Outhred was right: electricity restructuring is complex and never-ending; it is not a picture of stability punctuated by insightful reforms based on single studies. Instead, success in reform requires recognising the multiple facets of the ESI and its societal context and must be underpinned by an enduring consensus on the policy goals.

References

ACCC (2018a). *Retail Electricity Pricing Inquiry final report*, Australian Competition and Consumer Commission.

ACCC (2018b). *Retail Electricity Pricing Inquiry: final report June 2018*, Australian Competition and Consumer Commission.

AEMC (2017). *2017 AEMC retail energy competition review*, Australian Energy Market Commission.

AEMC and KPMG (2013). *The National Electricity Market: A case study in successful microeconomic reform*, Australian Energy Market Commission, Sydney.

AER (2017). *Media release: Market Bodies Forum launched*, 7 June 2017, https://www.aer.gov.au/communication/market-bodies-forum-launched.

Ajaz, W (2019). 'Resilience, environmental concern, or energy democracy? A panel data analysis of microgrid adoption in the United States', *Energy Research & Social Science*, vol. 49, pp. 26–35.

Allbut, G (1958). *A brief history of some of the features of public electricity supply in Australia: and the formation and development of the Electricity Supply Association of Australia, 1918–1957*, Electricity Supply Association of Australia.

Andersen, GF (1992). *Electricity supply in Doncaster and Templestowe: A history of the Electricity Department of the City of Doncaster and Templestowe*, City of Doncaster and Templestowe.

Anthony, RHD (1977). *National Energy Advisory Committee*, 10 February 1977, https://pmtranscripts.pmc.gov.au/sites/default/files/original/00004318.pdf.

Armstrong, PJ (2002). *From council to corporation: The history of Newcastle's electricity supply*, Shortland County Council.

Aulich, C and Wettenhall, R (2017). 'Policy and governance for electricity supply in Australia: Public or private interest?', *Journal of Contemporary Issues in Business and Government*, vol. 23, no. 1, p. 30.

Battellino, R (2010). 'Mining booms and the Australian economy', RBoA Deputy Governor, Address to The Sydney Institute, Sydney, 23 February 2010.

Beale, R, Houston, G, Kenny, P, Morton, E and Tamblyn, J (2006). *Expert Panel on Energy Access Pricing: Report to the Ministerial Council on Energy*, Ministerial Council on Energy.

Boehm, EA (1956). 'Ownership and control of the electricity supply industry in Australia', *Economic Record*, vol. 32, no. 2, pp. 257–72.

Booth, RR (2000). *Warring tribes: The story of power development in Australia*, Rev. edn, Bardak Group.

Borland, J (2015). 'Microeconomic reform', in SP Ville and G Withers (eds), *The Cambridge economic history of Australia*, Cambridge University Press.

Burke, MJ and Stephens, JC (2017). 'Energy democracy: Goals and policy instruments for sociotechnical transitions', *Energy Research & Social Science*, vol. 33, pp. 35–48.

Butlin, N, Barnard, A and Pincus, J (1982). *Government and capitalism: Public and private choice in twentieth century Australia*, Allen & Unwin, Sydney.

Carr, EH (1961). *What is history?*, Penguin UK.

Chester, L (2012). 'The Australian variant of neoliberal capitalism', in D Cahill, L Edwards and FJB Stilwell (eds), *Neoliberalism: Beyond the free market*, pp. 153–79.

COAG (2007). 'COAG National Reform Agenda (Competition Reform): Response to the Energy Reform Implementation Group'.

Commission of Inquiry into Electricity Generation Planning in New South Wales (1987). *Commission of Inquiry into Electricity Generation Planning in New South Wales: [report]*, NSW Government Printer, Sydney.

Committee, ANEA (1983). *Electricity in the Australian energy market*, Canberra.

Cornish, S (1993). 'The Keynesian revolution in Australia: Fact or fiction?', *Australian Economic History Review*, vol. 33, no. 2, pp. 42–68.

Darroch, S (2015). *Power for the people: An (uncensored) story of electricity in Australia 1770–2015*, ETT Imprint and The Svengali Press.

Dike, J and Lamb, PG (2012). *Torquay's electricity history: 1877–1948*, South Western Electricity Historical Society, Bristol.

Doran, C (1990). *Partner in progress: A history of electricity supply in North Queensland from 1897 to 1987*, Dept of History and Politics, James Cook University.

Edwards, C (1969). *Brown power: A jubilee history of the State Electricity Commission of Victoria*, State Electricity Commission of Victoria.

Edwards, R (2020). *Review of Energy Security Board*, Department of Industry, Science, Energy and Resources.

Electricity Advisory Committee (1945). *Recommendations of the Electricity Advisory Committee on the question of the co-ordination and control of electricity generation and distribution*, NSW Government Printer, Sydney.

ENA and CSIRO (2016). *Electricity network transformation roadmap: Key concepts report.*

Energy Ministers (2020). *ESB Review – Energy Ministers response*, Canberra.

Evans, T (2004). 'Early reforms in management and culture', in G Hodge, V Sands, D Hayward and D Scott (eds), *Power progress: An audit of Australia's electricity reform experiment*, Australian Scholarly Publishing, Melbourne, pp. 9–21.

Fathollahzadeh, R (2005). 'Electricity industry reform in Australia: Reasons, impacts, challenges', *UTS: Engineering Research Showcase*, UTS.

Finkel, AC (2017). *Blueprint for the future: Independent review into the future security of the National Electricity Market (Expert Panel on the Independent Review into the Future Security of the National Electricity Market)*, Department of the Environment and Energy, Canberra.

Fraser, M (1980). 'Election policy speech', Prime Minister, Campaign launch, Melbourne, 30 September 1980.

Garvie, RMH (1962). *A million horses: Tasmania's power in the mountains*, Hydro-Electric Commission, Tasmania.

Geels, FW (2002). 'Technological transitions as evolutionary reconfiguration processes: A multi-level perspective and a case-study', *Research Policy*, vol. 31, no. 8, pp. 1257–74.

Gibson, AJ (1929). *Report on power development in Australia*, Government printer, Canberra.

Harvey, C and Peckman, NJ (1993). *Yallourn Power Station: A history, 1919 to 1989*, State Electricity Commission of Victoria.

Hausman, WJ, Hertner, P and Wilkins, M (2008). *Global electrification: Multinational enterprise and international finance in the history of light and power, 1878–2007*, Cambridge Books.

Havyatt, D (2021). 'Australian electricity prices 1953 to 2020'. *Mimeo*, available at https://www.researchgate.net/publication/349992582_Australian_electricity_prices_1953_to_2020_v5.

Hawke, RJL (1990a), *Prime Minister's opening statement: Special Premiers' Conference, Brisbane 30 October 1990*, Australian Government.

Hawke, RJL (1990b). 'Speech, "Micro-economic reform: The fourth term agenda"', Prime Minister of Australia.

Hilmer, FGC (1993). *National competition policy: Independent Committee of Inquiry into Competition Policy in Australia*, Australian Government Publishing Service.

(IAC) Industries Assistance Commission (1989). *Inquiry into government (non-tax) charges: The electricity supply industry in Australia*, Commonwealth of Australia, Canberra.

(IC) Industry Commission (1991). *Energy generation and distribution*, Commonwealth of Australia, Canberra.

(IC) Industry Commission (1991). 'Costs and benefits of reducing greenhouse gas emissions', Commonwealth of Australia, Canberra.

(IC) Industry Commission (1995). *The growth and revenue implications of Hilmer and related reforms: A report by the Industry Commission to the Council of Australian Governments*, Commonwealth of Australia, Canberra.

Inchbold-Busby, S (2011). *The night the lights went on: The story of the first municipality in Australia to light its streets using electricity: An oral history and other stories from the Tamworth Powerstation Museum*, Tamworth Powerstation Museum.

Jones, HA (1980). *History of electricity in the A.C.T*, Institution of Engineers Australia.

Julius, GA (1926). 'Australian made: Presidential address', *Transactions of the Institution of Engineers, Australia*, Vol VI.

Julius, GA (1927). *Production efficiency*, delivered in part as an address before the Electrical Federation of Victoria, 25 November 1926, Institution of Engineers Australia.

Karmel, F (2018). 'Deregulation and reform of the electricity industry in Australia'.

Keating, P (1992). *Transcript of Joint Press Conference, Heads of Government Meeting, 11 May 1992*, Australian Government.

Kellow, A (1996). *Transforming power: The politics of electricity planning*, Cambridge University Press.

Kerr, C and Kerr, M (1979). *The vital spark: The story of electricity supply in South Australia*, Electricity Trust of South Australia.

Lincolne, GB (1955). *Electricity supply in Victoria*, State Electricity Commission of Victoria.

Linn, R (1996). *ETSA: The story of electricity in South Australia*, Historical Consultants for ETSA.

Low, RA (1992). *Switched on in the west: A history of electricity supply to Parramatta and the western region of Sydney 1890 to 1990*, Parramatta and District Historical Society.

Low, RA (2004). *Switched on in the Hunter: A history of electricity supply to Newcastle and the Hunter Valley 1889–1996*, EnergyAustralia.

McDonell, G (1989). 'Power supply, energy markets and national co-ordination: A critique', *The Australian Quarterly*, vol. 61, no. 1, pp. 4–16.

McKell, WJ (1945). *Electricity co-ordination in Great Britain and rural electrification in the United States of America, Great Britain and Canada*, NSW Government Printer.

McLaren, H (1994). *Electricity supply in Pinnaroo: A general history of events until the takeover by the Electricity Trust of South Australia in 1961*, HG McLaren.

McLean, I (2013). *Why Australia Prospered. The shifting sources of economic growth*, Princeton University Press, p. 147.

McLean, IW and Shanahan, MP (2007). 'Australasian economic history: Research challenges and big questions', *Australian Economic History Review*, vol. 47, no. 3, pp. 300–15.

Monash, J (1924). 'Presidential address', *Report of the meeting of the Australasian Association for the Advancement of Science*, pp. 1–36.

Moran, A and Skinner, B (2008). 'Resource adequacy and efficient infrastructure investment', in F Sioshansi (ed.), *Competitive electricity markets: Design, implementation, performance,* Elsevier, pp. 387–416.

Moran, A and Sood, R (2013). 'Evolution of Australia's National Electricity Market', in FP Sioshansi (ed.), *Evolution of global electricity markets*, Academic Press, Boston, pp. 571–614.

Morwood, J (1968). *History of electricity supply in Brisbane*, Institution of Engineers, Australia, Queensland Division.

Napier, G and Easdown, G (1993). *The Kiewa story*, State Electricity Commission of Victoria.

National Archives of Australia: Department of Prime Minister and Cabinet; A1209 (1991). '1992/1333, Reform of the Electricity Supply – Industry Branch; Electricity Generation and Transmission Interstate Co-operation Heads of Agreement'. Paper Files and Documents.

National Archives of Australia: Department of Prime Minister and Cabinet; A1209 (1992a). '1992/2363, Reform of the Electricity Supply Industry Branch; Memo from Rod Sims to PM Keating on National Grid Corporation'. Paper Files and Documents.

National Archives of Australia: Department of Prime Minister and Cabinet; A1209 (1992b). '*1993/243 Memo from Peter Harris; Electricity Reform – What May Need to be Done in Perth*'. Paper Files and Documents.

Nelson, T and Orton, F (2016). 'Australia's National Electricity Market: Optimising policy to facilitate demand-side response', *Australian Economic Review*, vol. 49, no. 2, pp. 146–68.

Newbery, DM and Green, R (1996). 'Regulation, public ownership and privatization of the English electricity industry', in *International comparisons of electricity regulation*, pp. 25–81.

Parer, WR (2002). *Towards a truly national and efficient energy market*, Commonwealth of Australia.

Pearson, L (2000). *History of the early electricity supply industry in the Cairns region, Barron River Hydro-electric Extension Project*, LM Pearson.

Pearson, L (2001). *The Hydro, the Barron Falls hydro-electricity board: History of the early supply industry in the Cairns region, Part 2*, LM Pearson.

Pearson, L (2007). *The history of the Cairns Regional Electricity Board*, 1st edn, LM Pearson.

Pearson, L (2010). *The history of the Cairns Regional Electricity Board – Part 2: Barron Gorge Hydro-Electric Extension Project*, L. Pearson.

Penrose, H (1995). *Bright sparks: The Brunswick Electricity Supply Department, 1912–1994*, Brunswick Electricity Supply Department, 1995.

Prentice, S (1982). *Electricity in early Brisbane*, Institution of Engineers Australia.

Productivity Commission (2003). *From industry assistance to productivity: 30 years of 'the Commission'*, Productivity Commission, Canberra.

Quiggin, J (1996). *Great expectations: Microeconomic reform and Australia*, Allen & Unwin.

Rai, A and Nelson, T (2019). 'Australia's National Electricity Market after twenty years', *Australian Economic Review* (online before publication).

Read, PC (1985). 'The organisation of electricity supply in Tasmania', University of Tasmania, Sandy Bay.

Rendel, Palmer & Tritton (Firm (1937). *Report on electrical development in New South Wales*, Rendel, Palmer & Triton.

Ruddock, JF (1981). *History of the Electricity Supply Department*, City of Melbourne.

Rusden, GF (1968). *History of Yallourn, Yallourn North and Yallourn North extension open cuts: July, 1947 to June, 1965*, Fuel Dept, State Electricity Commission of Victoria.

Santayana, G (1905–06). *The life of reason: The phases of human progress*, Volume 1: Reason in common sense, C. Scribner's Sons, New York.

Scales, BC (2007). 'Energy reform: The way forward for Australia. A report to the Council of Australian Governments by the Energy Reform Implementation Group'. Retrieved from energy-reform-way-forward-aust-final-report-exec-summary-2007_0.pdf.

Schweppe, FC, Caramanis, ME, Tabors, RD and Bohn, RE (1988). *Spot pricing of electricity*, Kluwer Academic.

Smith, N (1988). *Electricity in Queensland*, Queensland Division, Royal Australian Institute of Public Administration.

Spoehr, JD (2008). 'Losing power: The struggle for control of South Australia's electricity industry', University of South Australia.

Tait, PG (1925). *Tait's electrical directory of Australia and New Zealand*, 6th edn, Peter G Tait, Melbourne and Sydney.

Thombs, RP (2019). 'When democracy meets energy transitions: A typology of social power and energy system scale', *Energy Research & Social Science*, vol. 52, pp. 159–68.

Thomis, MI (1987). *A history of the electricity supply industry in Queensland. Volume I, 1888–1938*, Boolarong Publications for Queensland Electricity Commission.

Thomis, MI (1990). *A history of the electricity supply industry in Queensland. Volume II, 1938–1988*, Boolarong Publications for Queensland Electricity Commission.

Thornton, KD (2015). 'The Electricity Commission of New South Wales and its place in the rise of centralised coordination of bulk electricity generation and transmission 1888–2003', Doctor of Philosophy thesis, University of Newcastle.

van Veelen, B and van der Horst, D (2018). 'What is energy democracy? Connecting social science energy research and political theory', *Energy Research & Social Science*, vol. 46, pp. 19–28.

Vertigan, M, Yarrow, G and Morton, E (2015). *Review of governance arrangements for Australian Energy Markets final report*, COAG Energy Council.

Vines, JA (2000). *A history of the Loy Yang mine: Its origins and development to May 1997*, State Electricity Commission of Victoria.

Warrandyte Historical Society (2003). *Bringing electricity to Warrandyte, 1926–1935*, Warrandyte Historical Society.

White, J (1986). *Power in the east: A short history of the Electricity Department of the City of Doncaster and Templestowe*, City of Doncaster and Templestowe.

Wide Bay–Burnett Regional Electricity Board (1977). *A Wide Bay–Burnett Regional Electricity Board, 1946–1977: A history* (n.p.).

Wilkenfeld, G (2004). *Electrifying Sydney: 100 Years of EnergyAustralia*, EnergyAustralia, Sydney.

Williams, R (1983). *An electric beginning: A history of electricity supply in the Mackay region 1924–1983*, Mackay Electricity Board.

Zeidler, D, Sir (1981). *Committee of Inquiry into Electricity Generation and the Sharing of Power Resources in South-East Australia*, Australian Government Publishing Service.

Chapter 2

How Not to Reform
Electricity Transmission

Lessons from Australia

Stephen P. King[1]

Introduction

Australia's National Electricity Market (NEM) 'is a $200-billion machine that produces and sells electricity across five states with relentless precision, 24 hours a day, every day … [It is] smeared across 5000 kilometres of south-eastern Australia' (Warren 2019, Chapter 4).

Before the NEM started in 1998, electricity networks were integrated, state-owned-and-operated entities, based on engineering, not economics.

For example, in Victoria, the State Electricity Commission (SECV) was established in 1921 under the chairmanship of engineer and wartime leader Sir John Monash. It operated the entire Victorian electricity system – from the coal mines to the switchboards in factories and houses.[2]

By the 1980s, questions were being raised about the cost of this integrated model:

> The publicly owned vertically integrated monopoly utility, SECV, was not generating the maximum benefits for its citizens or customers. In particular a number of weaknesses had emerged such as poor capital

1   **Stephen P. King**, Productivity Commission, Melbourne, Australia.
     The views presented in this paper are those of the author and do not
     represent, and should not be attributed to, the Productivity Commission.
2   See https://www.secv.vic.gov.au/history/.

investment decisions, over capitalisation of assets, low levels of plant availability and inefficient work practices. (Fearon and Moran, n.d.).

In 1994 the SECV was broken into three separate entities covering mining and generation, transmission and security, and distribution and retailing.[3]

Other state electricity businesses followed a similar path. For example, the Electricity Commission of NSW was formed in 1950 as a government-owned monopoly covering the entire electricity system. The transmission system was separated and renamed TransGrid in 1995. TransGrid is now a private company that operates the transmission network in NSW, although the transmission assets remain under government ownership.[4] In contrast, SP-AusNet (now AusNet Services) acquired Victoria's electricity transmission assets in the late 1990s.

The restructuring of electricity networks and the creation of the NEM aimed to move Australia from an 'engineering focused' approach to electricity towards a 'market focus'. Rather than having engineers centrally plan new infrastructure, such as generation, these investments would be left to competition in a market and governed by price signals.

However, transmission always sat uncomfortably within this vision. Transmission networks are almost always considered to be natural monopolies.[5] In other words, it is cheaper to provide all relevant services through a single transmission network than multiple networks.[6] In such a situation, competition through a market is likely to fail, as larger providers can always under-price and drive out smaller competitors.

Such a view is clearly incomplete. Transmission systems can theoretically compete with each other; for example, when different transmission systems connect geographically separated generators to bring power to the distribution network in one urban centre. But the restructuring of transmission in Australia that preceded the NEM effectively ruled out this type of competition. Single government-owned or private companies control all the transmission in each state.

---

3   See https://www.secv.vic.gov.au/history/.
4   TransGrid, 'Our History', available at: https://transgrid.com.au/who-we-are/about-us/history/Pages/default.aspx#:~:text=The%20Electricity%20Commission%20of%20New,state's%20electricity%20generation%20and%20supply. Accessed 26 August 2020.
5   See Australian Energy Market Commission (2018) at p. 37 and Finkel, Moses, Munro, Effeney and O'Kane (2017) at p. 129.
6   For the formal definition of a natural monopoly, see Panzar (1989).

Transmission networks can also compete with local generation to meet power demand. But the historic structure of electricity networks in Australia involved generators located near fuel sources and long, stringy transmission systems bringing that power to the major urban centres. This structure continued into the NEM with market-based competition between transmission and generation investments effectively ruled out. While generation and transmission investments theoretically compete with each other, this is through a regulatory process that, in all parts of the NEM except Victoria, is initiated by the transmission network service providers (TNSPs) themselves and is evaluated by the Australian Energy Regulator (AER). This regulated cost–benefit approach has little if any resemblance to a market.

Transmission assets can also compete by connecting and arbitraging price differences between separated nodes within an electricity market. The NEM allows for transmission investments to operate on this basis, providing 'market network services'. In general, however, investors that establish transmission investments to arbitrage power prices have found it desirable to move to a regulated status. For example, Murraylink, a privately built interconnector between Victoria and South Australia, was brought into operation in 2002 as a provider of market network services. Almost immediately, however, it applied to be explicitly regulated (become a 'prescribed service') and receive a guaranteed regulated revenue rather than depend on the vagaries of the market.[7] Basslink, connecting Victoria and Tasmania, is currently the only unregulated interconnector. However, it operates under a long-term contract with the state government owned Hydro Tasmania, the main generator in Tasmania. Basslink operates as part of Hydro Tasmania to both manage water resources and to arbitrage prices so, rather than being driven by market signals, the interconnector is simply part of a broader generation operation.[8]

In summary, if restructuring in the lead up to the creation of the NEM had been done differently, then some form of competition in transmission may have been possible. But effective competition was ruled out by the way the NEM was designed.

This put transmission in an odd position. Transmission assets overwhelmingly receive a regulated return. But the owners of these assets have driven

---

7   Murraylink Transmission Company (2002), 'Application for Conversion to a Prescribed Service and a Maximum Allowable Revenue for 2003–12', October 18.

8   Thus 'from the outset, Basslink was intended to be used as a net supply option for Tasmania in times of low hydrological inflows (drought), as well as net exports in times of high inflows' (Pierce, Tamblyn and Fahrer 2012, p. 235).

new investment. Inevitably, this has led to a mix of cooperation and conflict between TNSPs and regulators. There has been excessive and uncoordinated investment that has been underwritten by consumers. And while TNSPs and the AER have a record of pricing disputes, TNSPs have been protected from, not exposed to, the market.

These failures of transmission investment within a market setting have inevitably led to a push-back towards a centrally planned, engineering-based solution. This has gained momentum in recent years with the Australian Energy Market Operator (AEMO) releasing a 2020 Independent System Plan that provides a centrally planned approach to the development of transmission networks in the NEM for the next twenty years.

However, this return to central planning is embedded within an electricity market and involves separated transmission companies that were designed and regulated for a market environment. The result is a system of transmission planning, payments and incentives that is 'neither fish nor fowl'. It is not a market system. But nor is it a centrally planned and controlled transmission network.

In this chapter, I will consider the state of transmission in the Australian National Electricity Market. In particular, I will consider the theoretical underpinnings for a market-based approach to transmission and show why, in general, this can be expected to fail. I will then discuss the regulated approach to transmission that operates in the NEM, and explain why it also has failed. Finally, I will consider the current mix of central-planning and market mechanisms for transmission, and the problems this raises.

Transmission in Australia's National Electricity Market

There are five main electricity networks in Australia. The NEM is the largest, running down the east and south-east coast of Australia, covering much of coastal Queensland, New South Wales, the Australian Capital Territory, Victoria, South Australia and Tasmania. Western Australia has two separate networks – the South West Interconnected System (SWIS) and the North West Interconnected System (NWIS). There is also the Darwin to Katherine Interconnected System (DKIS) in the Northern Territory and the Mount Isa–Cloncurry supply network (Mt Isa Network) in Queensland.[9]

---

9   Productivity Commission (2017). There are also local networks; for example, in Alice Springs and Tennant Creek in the Northern Territory. See Australian Energy Regulator (2020) at p. 117.

The discussion here will focus on the NEM as it is by far the dominant network in terms of power flows and customers.

The transmission networks in the NEM are operated by transmission network service providers (TNSPs). In Victoria the TNSP is a private company (AusNet Services) that also owns the network assets. In NSW (TransGrid) and South Australia (ElectraNet), private companies have long-term asset leases to operate the state government owned transmission networks. In Queensland and Tasmania, both the TNSPs and the transmission networks are government owned.

The state-based transmission networks are linked by six interconnectors. Three of these (Queensland–NSW, Heywood, and Victoria–NSW) 'form part of the state based networks, while the other three (Directlink, Murraylink and Basslink) are separately owned' (Australian Energy Regulator 2020, p. 117). As noted above, Basslink is the only 'unregulated' interconnector.

A TNSP that wants its transmission investment to be regulated must show that the relevant assets pass the regulatory investment test for transmission (the RIT-T) and be deemed as adding value to the NEM. From the TNSP's perspective, the benefit of regulation is the removal of market risk. Regulated transmission assets receive a regulated return based on a fixed-value asset base rather than face the vagaries of the electricity market. These regulated returns are built into the prices paid by consumers of electricity.

The RIT-T is a cost–benefit assessment that not only looks at whether the specific transmission investment adds value to the NEM but also whether it provides a greater net benefit than alternative investments in transmission and/or generation. The decision as to whether or not a transmission investment passes the RIT-T is made by the Australian Energy Regulator (AER). For example, the AER recently determined that a proposed South Australia–NSW interconnector passed the RIT-T. While the AER disagreed with some of the benefits included in the original RIT-T that was prepared by ElectraNet, it found that the (reduced) benefits continued to outweigh the costs. 'Residential customers in South Australia can expect to pay an extra $9 per annum and NSW customers $5 for the project but these costs will be more than offset by the benefits' (Australian Energy Regulator 2020a).

Over the past decade, renewable and other alternative sources of generation have gained increased prominence in the NEM. This is expected to continue, probably at an accelerated pace, in the next decade, creating two investment challenges for the transmission networks and the energy regulators. The first challenge is geographic. New generators, in general, are not located near traditional fossil-fuel reserves. Transmission networks need to be extended and enlarged to cater for these generators. Second, renewable generators provide variable power flows so that new investment is required to stabilise power flows in the transmission networks. In the next section I provide an overview of the theory underpinning the economics of transmission networks and show why this additional investment is unlikely to be forthcoming through simple market mechanisms. Rather, a regulatory solution will be needed.

The economic theory underpinning transmission networks

What does an economically optimal transmission network look like?

Transmission networks are the highways of the electricity system. They link the nodes in an electricity system, transporting power at high voltages from generators to areas of demand or 'load centres'. 'They consist of towers and wires, underground cables, transformers, switching equipment, reactive power devices, and monitoring and telecommunications equipment.'[10]

An economically optimal transmission network will sometimes be congested.

In theory, an electricity network could involve transmission links that are never congested. In such a situation, the links would be built to a capacity such that power flows never have to be constrained.[11] This implies that the spot prices for power at either end of any transmission link will be (close to) identical.[12]

However, transmission is costly to build and maintain, and power demand fluctuates significantly over time. An unconstrained transmission system would

---

10   Australian Energy Regulator (2020), p. 117. The transmission network links with the distribution network to reduce the voltage of the power and transport it to customers. While some large industrial customers connect directly to the transmission network, most consumers access power from the distribution network.

11   This is theoretical because, for there never to be any congestion at any time, the network would need to be built so that the failure or 'outage' of any set of elements in the system would not disrupt the power flow. Clearly that can never be guaranteed with certainty. Transmission capacity rules in the NEM are generally written in terms of reliability given planned or unplanned outages of network elements.

12   In the discussion here I will ignore transmission line losses and other factors that may lead to some small difference in spot prices. Our interest is in congestion that can cause significant differences in spot power prices across an interconnector.

be built with a capacity such that it could handle even very short periods of high power demand without congestion. Further, it would have its capacity increased over time to make sure that capacity is never reached even if the total demand for power is increasing.

Inevitably, at some point, the marginal cost of increasing the capacity of transmission to avoid any congestion is less than the marginal benefit of reduced congestion. This has two immediate implications:

- A least cost electricity network will sometimes have transmission congestion;[13] and
- When transmission is congested, there will be differences in power prices across the relevant transmission link.

To see this, take a simple example adapted from Stoft (2002, p. 391) of two nodes, A and B, that are linked by a single transmission line. Both nodes have generation capacity and have load or demand for power. For example, A and B could be different states where their electricity networks are joined by a single transmission link or 'interconnector'. Node A has low-cost generation that has a marginal cost given by $\$(20 + Q/50)$ per megawatt hour (MWh). Node B has higher cost generation with a marginal cost of $\$(40 + Q/50)$.

First, suppose that the (peak) load at A is given by 400MW and the load at B is 2000MW. Further, suppose that the interconnector had limitless capacity. At both nodes retailers will purchase power in the (competitive) power market for supply to end-users.[14] Retailers will purchase from either node A or B – whichever is cheaper. As there is no constraint on transmission capacity, we will assume that there is no transmission charge associated with power flows.[15] Then the spot market outcome involves a single price of power of $54 per MWh. Generation at node A will produce 1700MW, of

---

13   Thus, when considering transmission network congestion in the NEM, the AER notes that 'Not all congestion is inefficient, however. Reducing congestion through investment to augment transmission networks is an expensive solution. Eliminating congestion is efficient only to the extent that the market benefits outweigh the costs of new investment' (Australian Energy Regulator 2020, p. 163).

14   Formally, a retailer is an intermediary between the power market and the residential and business customer market. In practice, some parties, particularly those manufacturers with large power demands, could directly purchase power in the electricity market, depending on the exact market rules. However, we will refer to all 'purchasers' in the power market as 'retailers' for simplicity.

15   For example, the fixed cost of the transmission infrastructure could be recovered by end-user charges that are either separated from or added to the power prices paid by these end users.

which 400MW will meet local demand, while 1300MW will flow through the transmission link to node B. 700MW will be generated at node B which, when added to the power flow from node A, meets the 2000MW load at node B. The spot price paid for power, of \$54 per MWh, just covers the marginal cost of generation at both node A and node B.

Note that this distribution of load and transmission is the least-cost way of meeting demand. It will arise in the competitive spot market simply by generators being willing to dispatch additional power, so long as the price covers marginal cost, and retailers seeking to buy power from the cheapest possible source. The total revenue generated by the spot market to meet the level of demand for one hour will be \$129,600, while the total (variable) cost of generation and transmission will be \$95,800. There are inframarginal rents given by the difference between the total revenue and total variable cost, equal to \$33,800, with \$28,900 accruing to generators at node A and \$4900 accruing to generators at node B. These rents, for example, may contribute to the fixed costs of the initial generation investment.

In contrast, suppose that the load at A is given by 400MW and the load at B is 2000MW, but that the transmission link between A and B has a capacity limit of 1000MW. In this situation, it will not be possible for generators at node A to dispatch 1700MW of power with 1300MW (partially) meeting the load at node B. Rather, generators at A will be constrained to dispatch no more than 1400MWh of power to meet the 400MW load at A and 1000MW of the load at B.[16]

In this situation the marginal cost of power (and hence the price if the spot market is competitive) will be \$48 per MWh at node A. At node B there will be 1000MW of load that is serviced from local generation. The marginal cost (and competitive spot price) at node B will be \$60 per MWh. For one hour, the total revenue of generators at A is given by the spot price at node A (\$48 per MWh) multiplied by the dispatched load of 1400MW for one hour, which equals \$67,200. Generators at B sell 1000MW at the node B spot price of \$60, so they gain revenue of \$60,000. The total variable costs and inframarginal rents for generators at node A are \$47,600 and \$19,600 respectively. For generators at node B, the total variable costs and inframarginal rents are \$50,000 and \$10,000 respectively. There are also congestion rents. These are associated with buying 1000MW of power at node A for a total spot market

---

16   There are two main ways to constrain the relevant generators: either through the system operator limiting dispatch or by retailers expressing limited market demand due to them being unable to 'buy' transmission capacity.

cost of $48,000 and selling that power in the node B spot market for $60,000. The congestion rent is the gain made on this transaction, which is $12,000.

Transmission congestion has a number of features that are illustrated by this example:

- The existence of congestion on the transmission link leads to a divergence in spot prices at either end of the transmission link.
- The generators on the constrained dispatch side of the transmission link (node A) lose out because of the congestion. In this example their inframarginal rent drops from $28,900 in the absence of congestion to $19,600 with congestion. In contrast, the generators at node B effectively face less competition due to the congestion constraint and their inframarginal rent rises from $4900 to $10,000.
- The benefits to consumers go in the opposite direction to those of the generators. Consumers at node A buy their power at a lower price ($48 per MWh rather than $54 per MWh) when the transmission link is subject to congestion. However, congestion raises the spot price for consumers at node B, from $54 per MWh to $60 per MWh.
- The existence of congestion raises the variable cost of meeting the combined load at the two nodes, from $95,800 in the absence of congestion to $97,600 with congestion.
- Congestion leads to congestion rents. In this example, these rents are $12,000 for one hour. These rents will accrue to someone. However, who that 'someone' is depends on market design.

While the capacity constraint on the transmission link between nodes A and B leads to an increase in the cost of generating power to meet load, this does not mean that the existence of congestion is inefficient. There is a cost to reducing congestion and it is only beneficial to reduce or remove congestion if the benefits of doing so outweigh the costs.

To see this, suppose that the capacity of the interconnector could be increased to 1500MW. This augmentation would mean that the interconnector would not be constrained. It would be able to accommodate the 1300MW flow from A to B that is required for the unconstrained market outcome.

The augmentation would save $1800 in generation costs for every hour that the load at A is 400MW and the load at B is 2000MW. Suppose this occurs for 1000 hours each year on average and that for the rest of the time the interconnector does not face a capacity constraint. Then the augmentation would save $1.8m in generation costs per year. If the annualised cost of augmentation is less than $1.8m, then the augmentation can be justified on economic grounds. However, if the cost of augmentation is more than $1.8m, then it is cost minimising to not augment the transmission link and allow it to become congested for 1000 hours each year.[17]

Put simply, augmenting the transmission link to reduce or remove congestion is only desirable if the cost of augmentation is less than the loss caused by congestion – which in this example is given by the total increase in generation costs that arise due to the congestion.

Even if the transmission link could be augmented at a cost of less than $1.8m per year, that may not be the best way to reduce congestion. It may be more cost effective to reduce or remove the constraint by either investing in new generation capacity at node B or paying a customer whose demand is marginal during peak periods to reduce their load in those periods. For example, it may be cheaper to invest in limited peak-load generation capacity at node B rather than augment the interconnector. Such generation capacity may have a relatively high marginal cost and a limited capacity. As such, it may only be economic to run in peak periods. However, if the fixed cost of establishing the peak generation capacity is not too high, it may provide a lower cost solution to address peak demand at node B than augmenting the transmission link.

Who gets the congestion rents?

In the above example, there was congestion rent of $12,000 for each hour that the transmission link was congested. This occurs for 1000 hours per year leading to annual congestion rents of $12m.

These rents associated with transmission congestion will be collected by 'someone'. Who that 'someone' is depends on the design of the market.

The congestion rents could accrue to the owner of the transmission link. For example, the TNSP could buy power at node A and then sell it at node B. Its profit will be the difference in the spot prices less any transactions costs, multiplied by the amount of power that is bought and sold. Of course, these profits only accrue when the transmission link is congested, so that the spot price of power at B exceeds the price at A. The maximum amount of power that can be bought and sold in this way by the TNSP is simply the capacity of the transmission link. So, ignoring any transactions costs, the profits to the TNSP from such 'arbitrage' of spot price differences will be equal to the congestion rent.

---

17   In this example, demand is inelastic so there is no economic cost associated with changes in demand when local power prices change. Thus, we only need to consider generation costs in this example.

Alternatively, the congestion rents may be taken by the independent system operator (ISO). The ISO authorises dispatch in real time and can simply take the congestion rents as the difference between the payments in the two spot markets. The ISO may allocate these rents back to some market players – or do anything else with them that is allowed by the market rules.

Finally, private parties may be able to gain the congestion rents through either physical trades of power or through financial contracts. If a party has the 'right' to physically transport power over the interconnector then they can buy power at node A and transport it to B whenever there is a price differential. The maximum quantity of such physical transmission rights will be given by the capacity of the transmission link. Ignoring any transactions costs, the value of these rights will be equal to the congestion rents.

This physical process can be mimicked through financial contracts. For example, a simple 1MWh transmission congestion contract (TCC) for node B relative to node A simply pays the difference between the spot price at B and the spot price at A for the relevant hour.[18] In our simple example, this is zero if the transmission link is not congested and $12 if the link is congested. If there are 1000MWh of TCCs that are written, then the value of these TCCs is simply the same as the congestion rents. In other words, the private parties who hold the TCCs receive the congestion rents.

Of course, in the case of both physical and financial contracts, we need to consider who has the right to issue the relevant contracts. In both cases, the market price of the contracts will be bid up to their value: $12 per MWh when the transmission link is (predicted to be) congested and $0 when the link is (predicted to be) uncongested. So, it is the party that can write and sell the contracts that gains the congestion rents. For example, if the ISO sells 1000MWh of TCCs over a year, then the ISO will receive the total congestion rents of $12m. If the TSO can write and sell 'firm' transmission rights for the year, then it will be able to sell these rights for $12m.

Can congestion rents create a market solution for optimal transmission investment?

The existence of congestion rents suggests that a market-based solution to transmission investment might be possible. For example, if the owners of the transmission network, or third-party transmission investors, were allowed to keep the congestion rents, would this lead them to have incentives to invest

---

18   The idea of a transmission congestion contract was first formalised by W. Hogan (1992).

in network expansion to a socially optimal level? In other words, could the incentive to maximise congestion rents allow for a market-based approach that would lead to socially optimal transmission investment *if* these congestion rents were allocated to 'the right people'?

Unfortunately, the answer to this question is (in general) negative. Even if it is desirable for the transmission link to be augmented, that does not mean that, in the absence of regulatory intervention, a party who receives the congestion rents will have an incentive to carry out that augmentation.

To see this, note that in our example the congestion rents are $12m per year. In contrast, the additional generation cost of congestion is only $1.8m. The congestion rents exceed the generation cost which is the upper bound on the efficient cost of augmentation to the transmission system to remove congestion. So, it would seem as if there is 'enough money' in the system to fund optimal congestion augmentation.

However, that does not mean that there is a market participant that has the incentive to use those funds for efficient augmentation.

For example, suppose that the congestion rents are allocated to the TNSP. Unfortunately, rather than creating incentives for the TNSP to set a socially optimal capacity, such an allocation of rents simply gives the TNSP the incentive to maximise the rents. In other words, the TNSP will set a monopoly-level of transmission capacity. In our example, this would mean that the TNSP would seek to artificially constrain the transmission link. For example, if the capacity of the link is constrained from 1000MW to 800MW then congestion rents will rise from $12m per year to $16m per year.

So, if congestion rents are turned into monopoly rents by transferring them to the TNSP, the TNSP will seek to set capacity to maximise rents. Capacity will be below the socially optimal level regardless of its cost.

An alternative would be to pass the congestion rents to a third party who could build a 'merchant' link to augment the existing transmission link. Assume that a link, that would eliminate congestion, could be built for an annualised cost of less than $1.8m per year. Such augmentation is efficient, but a third-party who receives the congestion rents would never want to build such a link. The congestion rents will decrease as transmission capacity is augmented, so a third-party that received all the *existing* congestion rents would have no incentive to augment transmission.[19]

---

19   Formally, this is because in the example presented here, existing transmission capacity exceeds the monopoly level. If this was not the case then a third party would simply augment the capacity to the monopoly level.

Alternatively, suppose the third party only receives the congestion rents associated with any augmentation to capacity that they own. Then the third-party will have an incentive to augment capacity. However, this will be augmentation to maximise the congestion rents on the additional capacity. This will not be the socially optimal level of capacity augmentation.

In the particular example here, it is obvious that no market participant could be rewarded by real-time congestion rents to build the optimal level of capacity. If the optimal augmentation eliminates congestion, then the congestion rents disappear. The investor will receive no return for the socially optimal investment.

This is, however, a more general point. Congestion rents are maximised by limiting capacity below the socially optimal level. Even if optimal congestion from a social perspective involves some congestion rents, a private party who receives those rents will generally find it profitable to limit capacity below this socially optimal level.

It might be thought that this problem can be overcome by using forward sales of capacity; for example, through TCCs. If the third party were able to lock in the current congestion rents going forward, then it might be thought that this would overcome the problem of augmentation reducing those rents. However, such forward sales would not occur at the current prices if the buyers of the relevant contracts were rational. They would see the increase in supply of forward contracts as reflecting the proposed increase in transmission. If the market for forward congestion contracts is efficient, then any forward sales will simply reflect future actual congestion rents and result in the third party seeking to maximise rents.

In summary, despite congestion rents being more than enough to efficiently augment transmission in our example, there is no *simple* way to allocate those rents that will create the incentives for a private party to fund efficient network augmentation. More broadly, there is no *simple* way to create a market which will align private and social incentives for transmission investment.

Some form of regulatory intervention will be needed in order to get socially optimal transmission investment.

Regulation and transmission investment in Australia

The discussion above points to the problems of relying on markets to create incentives for transmission investment. This has been reflected in the NEM through the lack of market-based transmission investment. However, the regulatory approach that has underpinned transmission investment in the

NEM has also failed to induce socially optimal outcomes. Rather, it has led to overinvestment.

Transmission networks in Australia are regulated by the Australian Energy Regulator (AER). Traditionally the AER has used a form of rate-of-return regulation that is referred to as 'building block regulation'. This involves a number of elements. As with all rate-of-return regulation, it is based on a regulated asset base (RAB). The TNSPs are regulated to make a 'commercial return' on their RAB after taking into account depreciation and non-capital costs such as operations, maintenance and taxation.

The allowed revenue for a TNSP is set in advance, so a regulated network's returns rely on predictions of the future costs that will arise during the (five year) regulatory period. The TNSP also sets prices that aim to achieve that allowed revenue based on predictions about demand over the regulatory period. The AER reviews these prices annually to make sure that they are in line with the allowed revenue for the TNSP. However, to the degree that the cost or demand forecasts are imperfect, the TNSP will either 'over-' or 'under-' shoot their allowed revenue. This can then be adjusted at the end of a regulatory period.

The regulated return is a 'weighted average cost of capital' (WACC) that is (supposedly) based on the capital structure of an efficient benchmark business. Over time the RAB is increased to include new capital expenditure. While assets in the RAB are depreciated over time, reducing the size of the RAB, there is no ability for the AER to adjust the RAB to remove assets that are 'stranded' or otherwise excess to needs.[20]

Building-block regulation, like all rate-of-return regulation, has a number of well-known limitations. For example, to the extent that the regulated return compensates a TNSP for the actual costs it incurs, there are few incentives for the TNSP to operate efficiently. While the TNSP may be allowed to keep any cost savings for the remainder of the regulatory period before 'handing them back to customers', any cost-minimising incentives this creates need to be weighed against the ability of the TNSP to pad-out costs in ways that either raise company profits or provide benefits for company executives.

For example, a network business may raise profits by also owning an unregulated network services business. The services business may provide a range of operational services to the regulated entity at an inflated price. If

---

20   Australian Energy Regulator (2020), p. 161. For more details on the 'building
      block' approach to transmission regulation, see Australian Energy Regulator
      (2020), pp. 122–127.

the regulated entity is able to recover this inflated cost through its regulated revenue, then the joint profits of the regulated business and the unregulated (but wholly owned) services company can increase.

Even if attempts to raise profit are prevented by the regulator, managers can increase costs by raising their salaries or perquisites. Shareholders of the network business will have little concern about this cost padding if it is simply offset by higher allowable revenues. But, of course, TNSP managers gain at the expense of end-users.

The AER is well aware of these incentives for a regulated TNSP to raise its costs, and has been moving to external cost benchmarking over time to improve the efficiency of the regulation (Australian Energy Regulator 2020, p. 127). Benchmarking (or more broadly yardstick regulation) establishes a regulated TNSP's allowed costs using the costs achieved by other companies. This creates incentives for each regulated company to reduce its costs as it gets to keep the difference between the cost benchmark and its realised costs. But, as each regulated TNSP reduces its own costs, this reduces the overall cost benchmark.

Prior to 2017, however, attempts by the AER to move away from a relatively strict rate-of-return approach – for example, through cost benchmarking – were often thwarted by legal decisions from the appeals body (Australian Competition Tribunal) or the courts. These decisions over-ruled and 'unwound' innovative approaches adopted by the AER. 'From 2008 to 2017, network businesses and other parties applied for limited merits review of 33 of the AER's 52 electricity network decisions'; many of these appeals were successful, adding '$3.2 billion to network revenues' (Australian Energy Regulator 2020, p. 126).

Appeal rights were significantly changed in October 2017, freeing up the AER for regulatory innovation.

Overinvestment by TNSPs

Building block regulation also creates poor investment incentives for TNSPs. Again, this is well known for rate-of-return-style regulation.[21] If a regulated business can achieve a regulated return on capital that is above its actual cost of capital, then it faces strong incentives to substitute capital investment for other non-capital inputs. Investment expands the TNSP's RAB, and if it receives a WACC above the market cost of capital this effectively lowers the

---

21   See Averch and Johnson (1962), pp. 1052–106. For a summary, see Viscusi, Harrington and Vernon (2005), pp. 433–436.

cost of capital. At its most simplistic, if the TNSP invests \$1m in unnecessary capital and pays a cost of capital of 8% but receives a regulated WACC of 12% then it is able to raise its revenue by \$120,000 while its costs only increase by \$80,000.

This effect has been borne out in the NEM by the rapid increase in transmission investments from 2006 to 2015. During this period there was a '62 per cent increase in the value of the RAB (caused by surging investment)' (Australian Energy Regulator 2020, p. 133).

The AER has laid the blame for much of the overinvestment on the regulatory rules.

> Network businesses receive a guaranteed return on their RAB. For this reason, they have an incentive to over-invest if their allowed rate of return exceeds their actual financing costs. Previous versions of the energy rules enabled significant over-investment in network assets, which partly drove the sharp rise in network revenue from 2006 to 2015. (Australian Energy Regulator 2020, p. 136)

Overinvestment led to the AER introducing a new incentive-based scheme in 2015 that allows a TNSP to retain any capital underspend for the current regulatory period and then retain 30% of the underspend in the next regulatory period (Australian Energy Regulator 2020, Box 3.4).

Unfortunately, attempts to alter regulations to prevent gaming often open up new avenues for gaming. This is sometimes referred to as regulatory 'whack a mole' – named after the arcade game where a player attempts to hit random stuffed animals. Every time one is hit, another one appears.

The AER recognises that it is playing regulatory whack-a-mole. It has included additional provisions to prevent a TNSP either artificially inflating planned capital expenditure (then retaining the portion that is not needed) or delaying efficient investment (and retaining the expenditure savings). However, these provisions involve relatively heavy-handed interventions where the AER will revisit all investment at each five-year review to check that it is efficient, and will set incentives to try and offset any incentives to reduce quality of service by delaying investment. As in the arcade game, each attempt by the AER to improve regulatory incentives simply creates another problem that needs correcting.

The incentives for overinvestment are exacerbated by the inability of the regulator to adjust the RAB for assets that are not needed – either due to demand changes or regulatory gaming. The Australian regulatory framework does not have procedures that allow the RAB to be modified 'downwards' for investments that are excessive to need. Indeed, the RAB cannot even be adjusted for assets that are no longer of any use (i.e. are 'stranded').

In this sense, the TNSPs face a one-way bet. Once an asset is added to the RAB it cannot be removed. While the asset will depreciate over time, the TNSP will still earn a regulated return on the asset that is independent of whether it is used or useful. The TNSP is protected from standard market demand risks, despite the fact that the regulated WACC is based on a commercial rate-of-return that includes compensation for demand risk. In such a situation it is unsurprising that TNSPs have found it profitable to overinvest.

The overinvestment will impact the NEM for many years. As the AER notes, 'consumers will continue to pay for the over-investment in network assets from 2006 to 2013 for the economic lives of those assets, which may be up to 50 years' (Australian Energy Regulator 2020, p. 134).

Overinvestment, however, has not been uniform across the NEM. There are a variety of factors at play in different states.

Some of the increased investment was driven by stricter reliability standards imposed by the Queensland and NSW state governments (Australian Energy Regulator 2020, p. 133). For example, in 2016, the Independent Pricing and Regulatory Tribunal of NSW (IPART) reviewed the transmission reliability standards for TransGrid, the TNSP in NSW. It noted that:

> Historically the level of reliability provided by the NSW electricity transmission network has been high. This has, at least in part, been driven by reliability standards that were set without reference to the value customers place on reliability. (IPART 2016, p. 1)

IPART (2016, p. 1) recommended more flexible reliability standards that 'would provide the most value to customers'. It also noted that, because of the long-lived nature of transmission assets, consumers were unlikely to see the price benefits of changed reliability standards in the near future. Rather, improved reliability standards would 'start to move TransGrid's network planning and decision-making process away from investing to remove any possibility of outages, regardless of the cost, towards a process that takes better account of the cost of providing reliability and customers' willingness to pay for it' (IPART 2016, p. 5).

States also differ in terms of the ability of TNSPs to influence the investment in their own network. For example, while the AEMO provided demand forecast information to TNSPs in all states, in Queensland and NSW the transmission businesses themselves made the demand forecasts that underpinned new investment. This led to concerns that the businesses were systematically over-forecasting demand in order to raise their regulated asset base. In contrast, AEMO provided independent demand forecasts for Victoria (Productivity Commission, 2013, p. 6).

Similarly, network augmentations in NSW and Queensland were planned by the local TNSPs. While investment in NSW and Queensland is subject to the RIT-T, which requires a comparison between transmission and alternative investments, and the investment required approval by the AER, the process was driven by the TNSPs, lacked transparency and invited gaming by the transmission businesses (Productivity Commission 2013, p. 7). In contrast, in Victoria the AEMO was responsible for planning, directing and procuring augmentations. SP AusNet (now AusNet Services), the TNSP in Victoria, had little incentive or ability to engage in excessive investment (Productivity Commission 2013, pp. 10–11).

While the AEMO approach used in Victoria involved a regulator that lacked 'commercial pressures' to minimise costs, the TNSP-planned approach used in other states also lacked these incentives due to regulation. Indeed, it is reasonable to argue that having AEMO plan augmentations meant that a variety of distortions were removed from the planning process and led to better outcomes for Victorian electricity users.

Reforming the rules for transmission investment: The engineers strike back

These problems with transmission investment and system planning are well known. For example, the *Independent Review into the Future Security of the National Electricity Market: Blueprint for the Future* (the Finkel review) noted these problems and considered that improved system planning was a key pillar for reform of the NEM (Finkel, Moses, Munro, Effeney and O'Kane 2017, p. 122).

> Better **system planning** should see AEMO having a stronger role in planning the future transmission network, including through the development of a **NEM-wide integrated grid plan** to inform future investment decisions. Significant investment decisions on interconnection between states should be made from a NEM-wide perspective, and in the context of a more distributed and complex energy system. AEMO should develop a list of **potential priority projects** to enable efficient development of renewable energy zones across the NEM. (Finkel, Moses, Munro, Effeney and O'Kane 2017, p. 5, emphasis in original)

The review recommended that the AEMO should work collaboratively with the TNSPs and other parties to develop an integrated grid plan for the NEM transmission network (Recommendation 5.1.). It recommended that AEMO's role in transmission planning be enhanced (Recommendation 5.3) and that AEMO 'in consultation with transmission network service providers and consistent with the integrated grid plan' would set out priority projects across the NEM. In particular, these projects would need to take into account the increasing level of renewable generation in the NEM (Recommendation 5.2).

Following acceptance of the Finkel report recommendations, the AEMO prepared its first Integrated System Plan (ISP) in 2018. It followed up with an updated plan in July 2020 and aims to continue updates every two years.

The AEMO's objective for the 2018 ISP was explicitly to consider future investment in transmission and generation together, particularly including options that allowed for a significant reduction in emissions over the NEM (AEMO 2018).

While this 2018 ISP represented a clear shift in the approach to transmission investment in the NEM, the 2020 ISP is much more ambitious and establishes an agenda for network design in the NEM. It sets out a roadmap for transmission investment looking forward to 2040. By considering the costs and benefits of 'groups' of investments, it presents an 'optimal development path'. The objective is to 'minimise long-term total system costs … while meeting the NEM's reliability, security and emissions expectations' (AEMO 2020, p. 39). As AEMO (modestly) notes, '[a]s a rigorous whole-of-system plan, the ISP is a far more comprehensive and richer analysis than other comparable modelling exercises for Australia's energy future' (AEMO 2020, p. 21).

By itself, the ISP is simply a plan to guide network development. However, a series of changes to the National Electricity Rules aim to explicitly favour projects that are identified in the ISP and require the TNSPs to action these projects through the RIT-T process. To achieve this, the rule changes require that:

- Each 'actionable' ISP project will be associated with an identified need.
- Relevant TNSPs 'will be required to publish a Project Assessment Draft Report (PADR) by the date set out in the ISP (not less than 6 months after the publication of the final ISP), unless the AER approves a request for an extension' (Energy Security Board 2020, p. 4).

- The information on the actionable project provided in '[t]he ISP will provide the overarching cost benefit analysis and risk assessment that specifies the identified need and one or more credible options to be considered in the RIT-T' (Energy Security Board 2020, p. 4). While a TNSP will still be required to present the ISP project to the AER for approval, and can also present an alternative 'better option', the RIT-T process will be 'streamlined'.

In other words, TNSPs are required to respond to a 'need' identified in the ISP and, while they have some flexibility in that response, the work done as part of the ISP reduces the regulatory burden associated with the project identified in the ISP. Indeed, the Energy Security Board proposed rule changes make it clear that the board considers that the ISP process makes redundant the previous Last Resort Planning Power conferred on the AEMO.[22]

These changes mean that the NEM will move away from a decentralised planning process that, at best, paid lip-service to integrated generation-transmission planning, to a centralised system for transmission investment. However, this central plan is embedded in a system of separated networks that are supposed to be responding to market signals within a regulated framework. It also requires separate generators, who have a mixture of public and private ownership, to cooperate through generation investment that is in line with the plan.

Put simply, the ISP is a centralised engineering plan for the NEM that must somehow be implemented through a system that is built on disaggregation and decentralisation.

Who pays?

Regulated transmission charges in the NEM are generally paid by consumers of power as lump-sum charges.[23] This includes the new investments planned under the ISP. Requiring consumers to pay for the transmission network

---

22 'The Last Resort Planning Power (LRPP) currently confers on the AEMC the ability to direct a TNSP to undertake a RIT-T where the AEMC assesses that an expected inter-regional constraint is not being addressed by a TNSP ... The ESB proposes to remove the LRPP on the basis that it will be superseded by the actionable ISP framework' (Energy Security Board 2020, pp. 21–22).

23 Formally, there are some user specific charges. For example, a generator that requires transmission augmentations to connect to the transmission network (connection assets) will pay a 'shallow connection charge'. Consumer charges however apply to the bulk of charges for the 'shared' network.

is justified on the basis that transmission networks 'serve consumers' while connecting generators have no guarantee of dispatch.

> [B]ecause there is an obligation on transmission businesses to reliably supply their customers, *it is customers who fund investments in the transmission network* that enable export of energy from generators, and relieve congestion where necessary. The costs of the assets necessary to provide a reliable supply are recovered solely from load (that is, customers). (AEMC 2017, p. 1, emphasis in original).

For fixed and sunk assets, it makes little difference whether consumers or generators pay the lump sum transmission charges. However, it does matter when there is new investment in both the transmission system and generation. In such a situation, by not paying for transmission assets, generators may have incentives to undertake investments that, from the perspective of the NEM as a whole, are not optimal and may have NEM-wide costs that outweigh their benefits.

To see this, consider the development of electricity storage systems (ESS) such as grid-scale batteries and pumped hydro facilities. These facilities sometimes act as customers, drawing power from the network to either charge their batteries or to pump water from low-level to high-level storage facilities. But they also act as power suppliers, either by discharging the batteries or releasing water to turn hydro-electric turbines. In essence these facilities operate to arbitrage power prices – buying power when the price is low and storing that power to sell when the price is high.

There are two significant pumped hydro facilities in the NEM: the Snowy Hydro scheme and the assets of Hydro Tasmania. The Snowy Hydro scheme is currently being expanded under the Snowy 2.0 initiative. Once completed, the expanded Snowy Hydro scheme will be the 'world's biggest pumped storage plant'.[24] The expansion is partially funded by the Australian Government (Prime Minister of Australia 2019).

Both of these facilities require substantial transmission investments to underpin their future use as ESS. This raises two questions. First, given that the transmission investments will underpin the profitable operations of these facilities, is it desirable for the facilities themselves to face the cost of the

---

24   Power Technology (2020), 'Snowy 2.0 Hydropower Project, New South Wales', available at: https://www.power-technology.com/projects/snowy-2-0-hydropower-project/#:~:text=Snowy%202.0%20is%20an%20expansion,pumped%20storage%20plant%2C%20upon%20completion (accessed 30 July 2020).

transmission investments? Second, given that these bi-directional facilities are both consumers and generators of power, will they face these transmission costs under current NEM pricing rules?

In general, it is desirable for generation facilities, including ESS, to face the full cost of their operations. If these facilities involve joint generation and transmission, then, if the investors do not face the transmission costs that they create, uneconomic projects may proceed as they are privately profitable.

This is the case with Basslink, the existing interconnector between Victoria and Tasmania. As noted above, Basslink is an unregulated interconnector but can best be thought of as simply part of the Hydro Tasmania generation system. Having Basslink fully funded by the operations of Hydro Tasmania in the electricity market ensures that Hydro Tasmania faces the full cost of the power it generates.

The situation is more difficult for the Snowy Hydro scheme. The HumeLink transmission link will be built to facilitate Snowy Hydro's increased operations. However, it is not a link that is dedicated to the Snowy Hydro facility. Rather HumeLink is 'a 500 kV transmission upgrade to reinforce the New South Wales southern shared network and increase transfer capacity between the Snowy Mountains hydroelectric scheme and the region's demand centres' (AEMO 2020, p. 14). AEMO listed HumeLink as an 'actionable ISP project' in the 2020 ISP, meaning that it is 'critical to address cost, security and reliability issues' (AEMO 2020, p. 14). However, it is far from clear that HumeLink would be needed or would pass the relevant investment test in the absence of the Snowy 2.0 initiative. At a minimum, it would be desirable if the Snowy Hydro scheme faced the incremental cost – the difference between the transmission augmentations that are needed in the absence of Snowy 2.0 and the costs of HumeLink – so that it faced the full economic cost of its activities.

However, Snowy Hydro is unlikely to bear any of the costs of HumeLink.

The AEMC considered the issue of payment of transmission use of service (TUOS) charges by pumped hydro and other ESS in 2018. In its final report, the AEMC aligned itself with a view that had been expressed by the AEMO: 'The Commission's preliminary position aligns with that of AEMO's, i.e. if an energy storage system is a scheduled resource and can be constrained off the network, it should not be required to pay TUOS charges' (AEMC 2018, p. 105). The AEMC, however, passed the actual decision back to the AEMO, suggesting that the AEMO submit a rule change request to the AEMC that would make the payment rules clear.

In August 2019, the AEMO submitted this rule change to the AEMC. The rule change would clarify that bi-directional generators (ESS) would not be required to pay TUOS charges (AEMO 2019, p. 29). In other words, while they would continue to pay (shallow) connection charges, they would not be required to make any financial contribution to shared assets in the transmission network, such as HumeLink.

Part of the AEMO's justification is that an ESS will not get 'unrestricted access' to the network so developing and operating an ESS should not lead to augmentation of the transmission network. This means that 'not charging TUOS for an ESS will not increase charges to others' (AEMO 2019, p. 29). However, this rationale is clearly incorrect for HumeLink given AEMO's own statement in the 2020 ISP that the rationale for HumeLink is intimately related to the Snowy 2.0 project.[25]

Like HumeLink, the Marinus Link is largely being built to service a particular ESS. The link will connect Victoria and Tasmania providing a second and, potentially, a third cable in addition to Basslink. The AEMO has concluded that the Marinus Link will 'deliver net market benefits and support the energy market transition by accessing necessary large-scale and deep storage in Tasmania to increase network reliability, allowing more efficient generation sharing between Tasmania and Victoria, reducing generation dispatch costs, and adding 540 MW hosting capacity to the attractive wind resource' (AEMO 2020, p. 62).

The main purpose of the Marinus Link will be to allow for the expansion of Hydro Tasmania's ESS services. It will allow Hydro Tasmania to further arbitrage electricity prices and increase its profits. Given this, it would be desirable for Hydro Tasmania to bear (most of) the costs of the Marinus Link, as it does for the existing Basslink. However, unlike Basslink, Hydro Tasmania will likely pay little if anything of the cost of the Marinus Link. Rather, it will be paid for by consumers.

This has created a political problem for Hydro Tasmania and the Tasmanian transmission company TasNetworks. Under the traditional approach for allocating the costs of interconnectors, Tasmanian customers would pay a substantial share of the costs of the Marinus Link. This may mean that the Tasmanian state government, which owns both TasNetworks and Hydro Tasmania, does not allow the link to proceed. The state government (and Tasmanian taxpayers) effectively see a truer reflection of the economic benefits

---

25   AEMO's rule change proposal was still being considered by AEMO at the time
      of preparing this chapter.

of the Marinus Link than Hydro Tasmania. Taxpayers benefit from Hydro Tasmania's profits but these might be outweighed by the cost of the Marinus Link. From a Tasmanian perspective the economic benefits might not stack up.

To avoid this problem, TasNetworks has issued a discussion paper arguing that Tasmanian customers should not pay *any* of the costs of Marinus Link. Rather, it argues that the benefits are gained by other consumers in the NEM and that 'Tasmanian electricity customers would be no better off with Marinus Link in service'.[26] Of course, if this argument were accepted it would mean that Hydro Tasmania and its owners would be able to retain all of the profits from arbitraging electricity prices using the Marinus Link while avoiding all of the interconnector costs.

This is an extreme example of how the existing pricing of transmission in the NEM can distort generation decisions. However, it is not hypothetical – it is actually in play as this chapter is being written.

Conclusion: The trouble with transmission

Australia's National Electricity Market has a problem with transmission investment.

The NEM was established on the basis that price signals would be able to drive efficient operations and investment of the electricity system. However, for transmission, there was never a reason to believe that this would occur. The economics of transmission networks means that some form of regulatory intervention will be needed to create appropriate incentives for network investment. This was quickly shown to hold in the NEM as early attempts to create market-based transmission interconnectors were moved back into a highly structured regulatory system.

Transmission network regulation in the NEM, while originally envisaged as light-handed and incentive based, quickly devolved back to heavy-handed rate-of-return regulation.[27] Both theory and evidence from overseas experience showed that this type of regulation creates strong incentives for overinvestment.

---

26 TasNetworks (2020), 'Beneficiaries pay pricing arrangements for new interconnectors', Discussion paper, available at: https://www.marinuslink.com.au/wp-content/uploads/2019/12/attachment-3-cost-allocation-discussion-paper.pdf.

27 In Victoria, the requirement to use 'price based regulation' but not 'rate of return regulation' was set in the regulatory rules. This resulted in a dispute before the Victorian Supreme Court. See H. Ergas and J. Small (2001), 'Price Caps and Rate of Return Regulation', 17 May, available at www.greenwhiskers.com.au. The author of this chapter provided evidence in that matter that building-block regulation was a form of rate-of-return regulation.

That proved to be the case in Australia for transmission networks, at least until 2015.

The incentives and structures of the NEM provide little if any incentive for either efficient generation investment or coordination between generation and transmission investments. Generators are able to create costs for the NEM, including transmission costs, that they do not bear. As both the Marinus Link and HumeLink projects illustrate, these misaligned incentives continue today.

At the same time, the failure of coordinated transmission investment in the NEM has led to a push back. Led by the AEMO and embodied in the 2020 ISP and associated rule changes, the planning of transmission and generation has shifted from a market basis to a centrally-planned engineering approach. While this represents a return to the pre-NEM approach to electricity in Australia, such a move back to central planning may be an improvement on the status quo.

Even if central planning represents a theoretical improvement for transmission in the NEM, it is almost certain to fail. The ISP is a central plan with no central planner. No organisation has the mandate or ability to implement the 2020 ISP. Rather, it has to work within a system of separated businesses, many of whom face quasi-market mechanisms but are simultaneously constrained by a range of heavy-handed regulations. When combined with pricing systems that distort incentives, even the best plan for coordinated NEM investment is likely to fail because it will not be optimal for all the required parties who need to accept it.

The end result is that we have a system of transmission planning, regulation and incentives in the NEM that fails to provide appropriate outcomes for consumers.

A key question that faces government is how to move forward. If the NEM has failed as an effective market, at least with regards to transmission investment, does this mean that a fundamental shift to an alternative structure is required? And if so, what should that structure be? Or can the NEM be redesigned to improve incentives for investment for at least some parts of the NEM? And if so, what role will regulators play for transmission, recognising that simple market incentives will not drive appropriate transmission investment?

It is clear that, at least for transmission, the current system of overlapping, inconsistent incentives and responsibilities in the NEM cannot continue. However, it is far from clear that anyone knows how to fix the problems.

References

Australian Energy Market Commission (2017). 'Fact Sheet: How Transmission Frameworks Work in the NEM', July 18.

Australian Energy Market Commission (2018). 'Coordination of Generation and Transmission Investment', Final Report, December 21.

Australian Energy Market Operator (2018). 'What is the Integrated System Plan?' Media release, January 25.

Australian Energy Market Operator (2019). 'Electricity Rule Change Proposal: Integrating Energy Storage Systems into the NEM', August.

Australian Energy Market Operator (2020). '2020 Integrated System Plan for the National Electricity Market', July.

Australian Energy Regulator (2020). 'State of the Energy Market 2020', Melbourne.

Australian Energy Regulator (2020a). 'AER Approves South Australia–NSW Interconnector Regulatory Investment Test'. News release NR 02/20, January 24.

Averch, H. and L. Johnson (1962). 'Behavior of the Firm under Regulatory Constraint', *American Economic Review*, 52(5), 1052–106.

Energy Security Board (2020). 'Converting the Integrated System Plan into Action', *Recommendation for National Electricity Amendment (Integrated System Planning) Rule 2020 Decision Paper*, March.

Fearon, P. and A. Moran (n.d.). 'Privatising Victoria's Electricity Distribution', Institute of Public Affairs, available at https://ipa.org.au/wp-content/uploads/archive/pfampriv.pdf.

Finkel, A., K. Moses, C. Munro, T. Effeney and M. O'Kane (2017). 'Independent Review into the Future Security of the National Electricity Market: Blueprint for the Future', Commonwealth of Australia, June.

Hogan, W. (1992). 'Contract Networks for Electric Power Transmission: Technical Reference', Kennedy School of Government Working Paper, Harvard University.

Independent Pricing and Regulatory Tribunal (2016). 'Electricity Transmission Reliability Standards: An Economic Assessment', Sydney.

Panzar, J. (1989). 'Technological Determinants of Firm and Industry Structure', Chapter 1 in R. Schmalensee and R. Willig, eds, *Handbook of Industrial Organization Volume 1*, North Holland, Amsterdam.

Pierce, J., J. Tamblyn and J. Fahrer (2012). *An Independent Review of the Tasmanian Electricity Supply Industry, Final Report, Volume 1*, Electricity Supply Industry Expert Panel.

Prime Minister of Australia (2019). 'Historic Snowy 2.0 Plan Approved', Media release, February 26.

Productivity Commission (2013). 'Electricity Network Regulatory Framework', Appendix F, Canberra, June 26.

Productivity Commission (2017). 'Supporting Paper 11: Energy', in *Shifting the Dial: 5 Year Productivity Review*, Box 3.1, Canberra.

Stoft, S. (2002). *Power System Economics: Designing Markets for Electricity*, IEEE Press, New Jersey.

Viscusi, W.K., J. Harrington and J. Vernon (2005). *Economics of Antitrust and Regulation* (4th edn), MIT Press, Cambridge.

Warren, M. (2019). *Blackout: How is Energy-Rich Australia Running Out of Electricity?*, Affirm Press, South Melbourne.

Chapter 3

Backsliding in Australian Energy Deregulation

Lessons from the Past and Recommendations for the Future of Reform

Steven Callander[1]

1. Introduction

Economic reform offers much promise. Throughout the 1980s and 1990s, the pursuit of economic reform was the focus of the Australian Government and much progress was made. The apex of reform efforts was the forging of competition policy in 1995. The *Competition Policy Reform Act* of that year brought all market activities in the country under a single framework and set in train a series of deregulatory processes that provided the foundation for Australia's productivity improvements over the ensuing decades. As described by the first president of the National Competition Council, Graeme Samuel, it was 'the greatest bipartisan multi-jurisdictional agreement we have managed to achieve since Federation'.[2]

1   **Steven Callander**, Herbert Hoover Professor of Public and Private Management, Professor of Political Economy, Professor of Economics and of Political Science (by courtesy). Graduate School of Business, Stanford University, Knight Management Center, Stanford, CA.

    This project has benefitted from many conversations with Dana Foarta and Takuo Sugaya and relates to several joint projects with them that are in progress. I also thank the students in my class, 'Energy: Innovation, Policy, and Business Strategy' at Stanford GSB, for many discussions on these topics, particularly on the opportunities for renewable energy. Michal Michlin-Friedlander and Guillaume Roger provided many helpful comments.
2   Quoted in Kelly (2009, p. 121).

While much has been gained from this reform, progress has been less than promised. In many cases reform has stalled before being completed, and in several prominent industries the gains that were made have been reversed. Instead of pushing reform forward, legislation post-reform has reduced the pressure on market participants to compete vigorously. In some industries these reductions in competition are permanent as the government approved industry consolidation via takeovers and mergers.

This backsliding in economic reform has been evident in financial services, most notably in the banking sector, in retail pharmacies, in telecommunications, and in the market for electricity. The electricity reforms of the 1990s and the creation of the National Electricity Market are particularly illuminating. The national market was created quickly with the injection of federal funds to build the interconnectivity infrastructure, yet the implementation of the actual market reforms lagged behind and, as of writing, remains incomplete. The reforms that have been implemented have been substantial; nevertheless the gains they have brought have been more ambiguous. Household energy costs have not fallen as hoped. Rather, as indicated in Figure 1, the price of household electricity has accelerated faster than inflation and faster than other energy sources, such as automotive fuels. The increases are only matched by its equally troubled sister industry of retail gas, and prices in both industries have seen a particular acceleration after the financial crisis of 2008–09.

Figure 1: Australian household energy price indices vs CPI

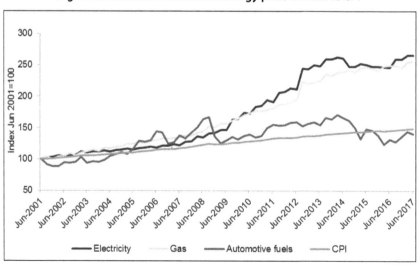

Source: Australian Bureau of Statistics (2017), Consumer Price Index, Australia, June 2017, 6401.1.

The slow incrementalism of reform has been paired on the market side with increasing market concentration. The original promise of reform was for competitive and distinct markets in energy generation and retail. The middle two stages, distribution and transmission, which still retain the characteristics of a natural monopoly, were to remain as a poles-and-wire regulated utility. Although initially there was an expansion of competition in generation and retail, over time both ends of the market have tended toward increased concentration. Moreover, both ends of the market are dominated by the same small set of players, namely AGL, Origin Energy and EnergyAustralia. The vertical integration of the so-called 'gen-tailers' represents a threat to market competition beyond concentration in market shares as it threatens the stability of the wholesale spot market for electricity, thereby making it difficult for 'naked' generators and retailers to operate effectively in the market. This evolution provides one possible rationale for the rising prices in Figure 1.

This problem is not unique to Australia. The much-lauded deregulation of telecommunications in the United States and the break-up of AT&T were promised to lead to a diverse marketplace and intense competition. Yet, the seven 'Baby Bells' that were produced ultimately were consolidated, with one of them, SBC Communications, eventually consuming the remnants of AT&T itself. While prices fell initially post-deregulation, the wave of mergers that swept over the market in the late 1990s and after has reduced competition to such a point that US telecommunications customers face some of the highest prices in the world (Philippon 2019).

In this chapter we explore the dynamics of deregulation. Why are well-intentioned reforms reversed? Under what circumstances do they stick? And, most importantly, what can be done about it? The answers we explore to these questions lie in politics. Deregulation is inherently a political process, but all too often the political questions – and the political will necessary for reform – stop at the point industry deregulation is executed.

Once implemented, however, the politics of market competition change. The economic incentives change, the politicians themselves often change, and, by explicit design, the set of interested firms changes. To understand deregulatory efforts, and to design them more effectively, we must understand this dynamic interaction of markets and politics. In this chapter we bring to bear recent work at this nexus and draw out the implications for economic reform. We apply these insights to electricity deregulation, looking backward at past failures and looking forward to the evolution of clean energy. We offer advice on how the policy failures of the past can be avoided and the opportunity of clean energy can be grasped through robust policy design.

At some level, the argument that politics matters is banal. But it is fundamental, and we need to go beyond the banality to understand why it matters and what can be done about it. It is also banal to say that competition is important to the success of deregulation. But no competent policy maker would execute a reform without a thorough economic analysis of market competition (typically a *dynamic* model of competition) to understand when competition is likely to emerge and how it can be successfully induced. The objective of this chapter is to do the same for the political economy aspect of reform: to analyse more rigorously when some reforms are reversed whereas others aren't, and what can be done in the design and implementation of deregulation to manage the political part of the process most effectively. For a policy maker to ignore political economy considerations is an abrogation of responsibility, and waving one's hands in lament that politics will inevitably undermine reform is not much better.

In formalising the political economy aspect of the economic reform debate in Australia, we hope to change the frame of debates around economic reform such that political considerations are placed on the same footing as the market competition considerations in setting the policy course. A new wave of reform in Australia is often spoken about as necessary and coming soon. For this wave to be more successful than the last, it must allow for not only market dynamics but also the dynamics of politics and how they interact.

Key takeaways

Approach and conclusions

We report, apply, and extend recent theoretical work at the intersection of political economy and industrial organisation – the academic fields that study politics and markets, respectively. In the model, policy makers decide whether to deregulate an industry and, if they do, new firms enter the market. Rather than stopping there, however, we analyse how competition evolves from that point. In particular we allow for firms to merge and for the industry to consolidate, but that consolidation is subject to political approval. The firms can lobby policy makers for this approval, sharing rents with them. The intention is to study this lobbying and market consolidation, and then to back up from there to evaluate the logic and wisdom of the decision to deregulate in the first place that sets this chain of behaviour in motion. By studying the co-evolution of these two markets – the product market and the market for political influence – we aim to shed light on each and on how their interaction affects market outcomes and political decisions.

74

The predictions of the model match the patterns of market evolution post-deregulation. In particular, the model is able to rationalise the cycles of market entry and competition that ultimately unwind, reducing competition and, in some instances, producing dominant monopolies. In fact, we show that the degree of entry and competition that immediately follows deregulation is greater than it otherwise would be precisely because competition will not persist. In rationally anticipating market consolidation, and the excess profits it brings, more firms enter the market than is socially efficient in the hope that a predator firm will successfully lobby the government and buy them out.

Policy implications

This modelling exercise yields rich implications for policy design and institutional structure. The immediate implication of the model is that the unwinding of the initial burst of competition from deregulation is predictable, and the model provides thresholds on the structural parameters of the market and of politics when it is more likely to happen. The key result is that there is a minimum degree of market competition that must be attained for that competition to stick and persist. Levels of competition that fall short of that will only succumb to lobbying and industry consolidation.

Backing up from this conclusion, the implication is that deregulation should not be attempted when the key threshold is not met. There will be industries, therefore, in which the basis of natural monopoly will have disappeared and that on economic grounds can support a satisfactory degree of competition, yet shouldn't be deregulated because the political process cannot offer the protection from consolidation that will lead to outcomes worse than the regulated market. This dichotomy – between markets that can sustainably support competition post-deregulation and those that can't – resonates with the Australian experience. The still large costs of entry in the generation market could not support sufficient competition, and has unwound (or has unravelled). The retail segment, with low costs of entry, was able to generate a sufficient level of competition. However, in allowing the largest retailers to escape that competition by vertically integrating and to use the leverage of integration to suppress retail competition, that segment of the market has been put on a similar path of consolidation and there is a lack of rigorous competition across the value chain.

The failure of deregulation to produce robust markets in generation and retail is an error that is difficult to unwind. Indeed, it is nigh on impossible at this point without the government imposing significant structural remedies on the industry. The rise of renewable energy provides a serendipitous opportunity to rectify this wrong – above and beyond the environmental benefits renewable energy promises for the planet. The age of utility-scale renewable energy is upon us. Yet the scale of renewable production is less than that of non-renewables and the cost of entry substantially lower. It is likely that the market for renewable energy will sustain the degree of competition necessary for it to be robust to political pressures. For this flourishing to take place, however, political pressures must be resisted now. Our recommendation is that non-renewable electricity producers be restricted, if not prohibited, from operating renewable plants, despite the obvious synergy such crossover would bring. This restriction on competition, counter-intuitively, is the best hope for competition to flourish and persist.

2. The economic logic of deregulation

To understand deregulation, one must begin with an understanding of why the industry was regulated in the first place. There are several possibilities, although for simplicity and relevance we focus on natural monopoly. Natural monopoly is the rationale underpinning regulation of the electricity industry as well as many other industries.[3]

A natural monopoly is an industry in which high costs of entry, returns to scale relative to the size of the market, or some other barrier to entry, give the largest supplier in an industry an overwhelming advantage over potential competitors. This characterised the electricity industry from its inception and through the first hundred or so years of its development.

Elementary economics tells us that a market controlled by a monopolist is inefficient. Not only will prices remain high but only a fraction of consumers will be served, leaving much consumer surplus untapped. One of the founding fathers of the electricity industry, Samuel Insull, appreciated that such an outcome would create problems for the operator, problems not in the market but with the government. He appreciated that having a product that could add such value – as electricity did – and to not make it available to the broader community would lead to a public backlash and a political response.[4] This fear was particularly acute in Insull's Chicago, where the memory of the Great Chicago Fire was fresh, and the ability of electricity to banish the need

---

3   Regardless of the motivation for regulation, the ideas we explore here are relevant to the logic of deregulation. We take up these possibilities briefly later in the chapter.

4   See Fox-Penner (2014) for a detailed account of this episode.

for the open flame of a candle would bring safety and not only convenience to the masses.

The genius of Insull was to be proactive in solving this problem. Rather than maximise profit and wait for the government to intervene, Insull approached the government and proposed a solution. That solution was the genesis of the regulated monopoly.

Insull proposed to the government that they regulate his firm, Chicago Edison (a precursor to Commonwealth Edison), and mandate universal service and price controls. In return, Insull obtained a government guarantee of monopoly – entry and competition in the market would be prohibited. This provided a cushy existence for the regulated monopolist.[5] The government-guaranteed monopoly was valuable not primarily thanks to the protection against the threat of entry (as the barriers erected by natural monopoly would usually be sufficient). Rather, the government guarantee was valuable as protection against future innovation, innovation that could displace the incumbent operator – what we would today call disruptive innovation.

The regulated monopolist has its advantages for society, yet it also has its costs. Not only would future entrepreneurs have a hard time bringing innovations to market, but the regulated monopolist would have a diminished incentive to innovate itself. More prominently, the incentive of the monopolist to keep costs down in a 'cost-plus' regulatory framework is minimal.

These costs and benefits, as well as the net outcome, can be seen most clearly in the classic supply–demand curve of introductory economics, as depicted in the two panels of Figure 2 (p.78). The left panel depicts the unrestrained profit-maximising market monopolist. With marginal cost, mc^M, it sets price at p^m to maximise profit, given by shaded region A. The inefficiency of this outcome is the missed potential consumer surplus, given by the solid region B.

The regulated monopolist is depicted in the right-side panel. The absence of market incentives leads to higher marginal costs, mc^R, but a lower regulated price and more consumer surplus. These simple figures show how the regulated monopolist, despite the inefficiency, can outperform the market when that market would be dominated by a monopolist. Nevertheless, the regulated monopolist is far from first best. Consumer surplus is still left uncaptured, and the inefficiency of regulation is avoidable (also not included here is the direct costs of regulation – namely, the regulatory agency that monitors the monopolist). This loss of potential surplus is given by the shaded area, R.

---

5   Insull also anticipated that the great scale required by universal service would make his operations even more efficient and lower his average cost even further.

Figure 2: Market outcomes for monopolist when unregulated (left) and regulated (right)

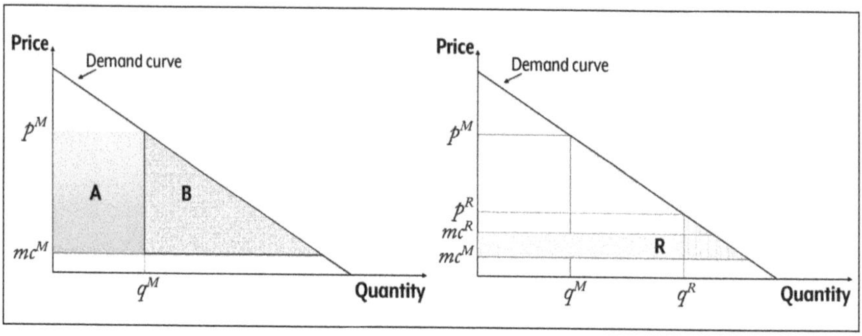

Source: Author.

The solution of a regulated monopolist worked imperfectly but reasonably well in cities and regions around the world for over 100 years. The necessity of this solution has faded in recent times. The growth of market demand, along with the construction of transmission lines that carry electricity over thousands of kilometres – such as in Australia's NEM – has expanded the size of markets relative to the optimum scale of power generation plants. Moreover, with more efficient production techniques the efficient scale of a plant declined rather than increased. These developments provided the economic case for deregulation.

More precisely, these developments provided the case for partial deregulation of the electricity industry. The transmission and distribution stages of the value chain – the poles and wires – remain natural monopolies and are regulated in Australia and elsewhere in the world. It is the ends of the value chain, power generation and electricity retail, where the case for natural monopoly has disappeared. Australian policy makers have led the way in bifurcating the value chain and deregulating both ends, whereas most jurisdictions that deregulated have concentrated solely on the generation end of the market.

The case for deregulation can also be seen via elementary economics, as depicted in Figure 3. The shape of the market is dictated by the number of generation plants that can be supported. The figure depicts two possibilities, one with four generators and the other with eight.[6] These outcomes are overlaid on the monopolist outcome. As is evident, the deadweight loss of surplus missed is smaller than the monopolist in both cases, and is decreasing

---

6   We suppose Cournot competition in representing market outcomes.

in the number of firms in the market (with eight firms the deadweight loss is region Y and with four firms it is Y plus Z). This is the classic intuition of market competition: the more firms that compete, the lower are prices, and the greater is the total surplus obtained (i.e. the more efficient is the market).

Figure 3: Market competition with four and eight firms

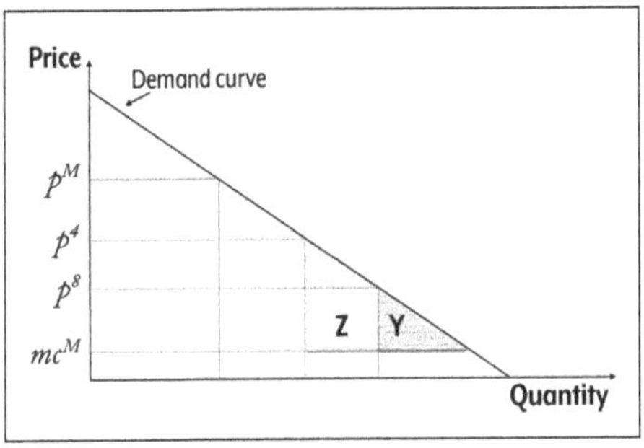

Source: Author.

Does the deregulated market do better than the regulated monopolist? That is less immediate, although the potential advantages are clear. The comparison depends crucially on the number of firms that enter and compete in the market. If deregulation does not obtain the degree of competition that is possible given the new efficient scale of production, then deregulation may itself even be a mistake. It is in this frame of reference that we turn now to the analysis of deregulation and market competition.

3. Why deregulation fails

The economic case for deregulation is clear: the end of natural monopoly in generation and retail is such that the market has the potential to support enough firms to make the efficiency gains worth the cost. The question is, however, will this rosy outcome actually come to pass? Will enough firms enter the market, and remain in the market, such that the gains from deregulation are realised? To answer these questions, we need to understand the initial post-deregulation phase in which firms enter the market and also the ongoing evolution of the market, to understand whether market competition emerges and also whether it sticks.

In a recent paper, Callander, Foarta, and Sugaya (2022) develop a model that captures this setting. They begin with the classic model of Cournot competition – in which firms choose quantities to take to market and are price takers – with fixed entry cost, $K > 0$.[7] They then add politics. Post-entry, one of the firms is empowered to lobby the government to be allowed to take over one of its competitors, at a cost of $L > 0$ per takeover. They show that it matters in this setting how many takeovers the predator firm can perform at once – capturing the speed at which a firm can *roll up* an industry – so let that limit be m competitors per period. If at the start of a time period there are n firms and the predator takes over x of them, then Cournot competition continues with $n - x$ firms. The model assumes that the predator firm must pay the target the fair market value of the firm.

To understand this model, and its predictions for deregulation in practice, one must proceed in reverse. We begin with an analysis of how the market evolves post-deregulation – the stage of potential takeovers – and then, from there, step back to the decision of firms to enter the market. Only then do we arrive at the initial decision to deregulate and are able to evaluate its full logic.

Takeovers

The motivation for takeovers in this setting is one that is present in every market: it reduces competition. By taking over some competitors, there are fewer firms in the market, and the profit of each firm goes up. This intuitive property is captured cleanly by the Cournot model of market competition. Figure 4 depicts the per-firm profit in one time period in a market with n competitors. It shows that profit is decreasing in the degree of market competition or, conversely, increasing in market concentration.

Figure 4: Per-firm profit from market competition

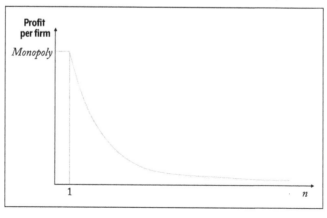

Source: Author.

---

7   Such as is used in Mankiw and Whinston (1986).

As intuitive as this relationship is, it does not mean that takeovers are always profitable. The acquired firm has to be compensated for forgone profits. The predator firm has to bear that cost itself, yet, as Figure 4 indicates, all of the market participants benefit from the reduction in competition. The predator firm, therefore, pays the cost of reducing competition but captures only a part of the benefit. The benefit spills over to the other market participants.

What matters, then, is the cost of acquisition versus the marginal gain in profit from removing one competitor from the market. It is evident from the shape of the curve in Figure 4 that the marginal gain of removing a competitor is increasing in the degree of concentration.[8]

It is also true that the cost of an acquisition is increasing in the degree of market concentration – as the forgone profits are then higher. Some straight-forward algebra establishes that this effect is dominated by the increase in the marginal gain of reducing competition. Thus, the incentive for a predator firm to acquire a competitor is increasing as market concentration increases. This calculation also implies that the appeal of takeovers is increasing in the number of competitors that can be acquired at a time as the price remains the same, whereas the benefit is increasing in each additional firm.

This discussion leads to the following conclusions on takeovers in the market.

Conclusion 1: *The profitability of a takeover is:*
(i)   *decreasing in the number of competitors.*
(ii)   *increasing in m, the number of competitors that can be acquired at a time.*
(iii)   *decreasing in the cost of lobbying, L.*

The payoff from this simple model is in what it implies for the long-run state of market competition. It delivers the striking implication that long-run market performance is bifurcated according to the number of initial competitors in the market. There is a threshold level of market competitors, $\hat{n}$, such that if the initial number of firms is at $\hat{n}$ or above, then no takeovers are made and the initial degree of market competition persists indefinitely. Below this threshold, however, industry consolidation occurs. In fact, not only are there some mergers, but the predator firm acquires all of its competitors and the market backslides completely to a monopoly state. This bifurcation is depicted in Figure 5. The left panel represents the number of takeovers given the initial number of competitors and the right-panel the final market structure.

---

8   See Salant, Switzer and Reynolds (1983) for the classic model of mergers in a
       Cournot framework.

Figure 5:
(i) Number of takeovers as function of competition,
(ii) Final market structure after takeovers

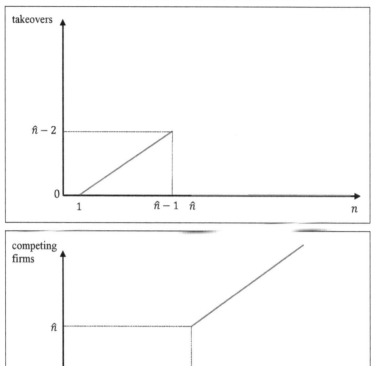

Source: Author.

The reason why markets separate in this way, and why backsliding is so extreme, is that takeovers are not only less profitable as the number of competitors increases; they are unprofitable beyond a threshold. At some level of market competition, the predator firm opts not to acquire its competitors even if it is allowed. When it doesn't, competition persists and the market stabilises at a high degree of competition. When the predator chooses to acquire a competitor, however, the appeal of further takeovers only increases, and the predator continues to acquire as many competitors as it can as soon as it can. This puts the market on an inexorable path to monopoly. We collect these properties in the following.

Conclusion 2: *There exists a threshold number of firms, $\hat{n}$, such that if the initial number of firms n is at least $\hat{n}$, there are no takeovers. If the initial number of firms is less than $\hat{n}$, the predator firm acquires the maximum number of competitors in each time period and the market converges on monopoly. The threshold $\hat{n}$ is decreasing in the lobbying cost, L, and increasing in m, the number of competitors that can be acquired in each period.*

The implication of Conclusion 2 is that market competition is sustainable if and only if the degree of competition is above a certain threshold. If competition cannot initially reach this threshold, it does not stick and the market backslides. This dynamic captures the backsliding that has been observed in practice following deregulations around the world.

Market entry

For the model to explain backsliding, it must also explain why firms enter the market in the first place even if they know that market consolidation will occur. This, it turns out, follows easily from the model. In fact, the model shows that entry occurs not despite the subsequent takeovers but because of them, and that there is excess entry into a market in which firms anticipate consolidation.

In the classic model of market entry (without subsequent takeovers), entry depends on the entry cost, K, and the structure of the market (demand and costs of production). The level of entry is decreasing in K and exceeds, if only slightly, the socially efficient level.[9] Higher levels of K correspond to industries with large fixed costs, such as electricity generation. Even with developments in electricity production, building a power plant is very costly. The retail electricity market stands in contrast, where innovations in information technology have significantly lowered the costs of entry.

Denote this level of firm entry as a function of K by $n(K)$. The prospect of takeovers and industry consolidation does not diminish this level of entry and, in fact, entry often exceeds it, as stated in the following.

Conclusion 3: *Market outcomes are described by two cases.*

(i)   *When $n(K) \geq \hat{n}$, $n(K)$ firms enter the market and competition stabilises at that level.*

---

9   See Mankiw and Whinston (1986). Entry exceeds the social optimum: the new entrant induces incumbents to reduce their production, as compared to before the entry. Therefore, entry is more valuable to the new entrant than it is to society.

(ii)   *When n (K) < n̂, the number of firms that enter is n*, where n* is at least n (K) and often strictly more, but less than n̂. The level of entry n* is decreasing in m, the number of firms that can be taken over in a single time period.*

Why do firms enter if they know they are to be bought out? And why does this entice even *additional* entry to what would normally occur? The reason is that the market with consolidation is more profitable than is the market without. Because the market will ultimately reach monopoly, profit in the industry is higher than it would be if competition persisted (although consumer surplus and total efficiency will be lower). Firms enter to get a piece of this larger pie. The firm that wins and becomes the monopolist clearly benefits. What is less immediate, but nevertheless robust, is that the other firms also win if one of two conditions is satisfied. The first is if there is uncertainty as to which firm will be the predator and attain monopoly, then more firms will enter in the hope of becoming the predator.[10] The second is if takeovers are spread out (the takeover constraint, m, is less than the number of potential competitors). This induces more entry because each time the number of competitors decreases, the profit of the remaining firms increases, and, consequently, the price needed to buy them increases. This implies that the expected purchase price for an entrant is higher when consolidation is slower, and this induces additional entry. The amount of excess entry is constrained, however, by the threshold, n̂, from Conclusion 2. If so many firms enter initially such that this threshold is breached, then it is no longer in the interests of the predator firm to take them over. There are too many competitors to buy and it is not worth even the prize of monopoly.

The decision to deregulate

Stitching the conclusions together provides an explanation for why, after deregulation, there is a burst of entry that is subsequently unwound, and why this pattern is rational for the firms. That it is rational for the firms also implies it is predictable for the policy maker. This predictive power is valuable as the cycle of entry and exit is inefficient. Many firms incur the cost of entry only to subsequently exit and abandon that cost. As the industry ultimately returns to monopoly, this means that the cycle of entry and exit is strictly inefficient.

---

10   The timing of when this uncertainty is resolved is also important for the takeover threshold, n̂. We explore the policy implications of this property in a later section.

Conclusion 4: *Deregulation that leads to entry and consolidation is strictly more inefficient than is transitioning directly to monopoly control of the market.*

This result shows that the lower bound on the efficiency of deregulation is quite low. It is worse, in fact, than simply allowing the regulated monopolist to transition to an unconstrained market monopolist. The firms are willing to pay the entry cost as entry allows them to extract a piece of the surplus inherent in a monopolist, but those entry costs are a deadweight loss for society.

It is important to observe here that in the limit – when entry is unconstrained by the threshold $\hat{n}$ – even the entering firms gain little from the cycle of entry and exit. Because entry is unconstrained, firms continue to pile into the market, paying the entry cost, until the point is reached that the cost of entry outweighs the value that can be extracted in a takeover by the eventual monopolist. The entering firms dissipate the surplus in entry costs in the pursuit of the monopoly profit. The only surplus they can gain is due to integer effects: the equilibrium is such that it is profitable for the n^*th firm to enter but not the $(n^* + 1)$th firm.

Corollary 1: *When entry is unconstrained by $\hat{n}$, the equilibrium number of firms that enter, n^*, is such that the expected profit for the $(n^* + 1)$th firm to enter is zero or strictly negative.*

Deregulation of industries often leads to bursts of entry and competition. When that occurs it is tempting to declare the deregulation a success. The important takeaway from these results is that to do so is a mistake. The burst of entry may be ephemeral and, indeed, the burst itself might be so strong precisely because competition is only temporary. Subsequent consolidations cannot be attributed to independent forces or be glibly blamed on politics. They are of a piece with the deregulation itself, and the wisdom of a deregulatory policy must be evaluated through this longer lens of time. In the following sections we turn to the policy implications of these conclusions and lay out possibilities for how they can be overcome or, at least, mitigated.

4. Policy implications and recommendations

One response to the preceding analysis is that takeovers and mergers simply should be prohibited. That once firms enter, they cannot reduce competition by combining. Within the confines of the model, that is certainly true. But in practice, firm mergers and takeovers are a vital part of a thriving economy.

An economy that is stable does not innovate and grow. Prohibiting takeovers and mergers is not a viable solution.

The question then is when they are allowed to occur. It is equally easy to say that mergers should only be approved when they are efficiency enhancing and not anti-competitive. These questions are easily answered in abstract theoretical models but, again, not so easy in practice. In practice, the market impact of a merger is often difficult to measure ex post, and ex ante must be predicted via imperfect economic models and fallible economists. It is, as a result, subjective, and good policy demands some discretion for those charged with implementing competition policy. Once there exists discretion, however, the door opens for political pressure. Alan Fels, an essential figure in Australian economic reform, identified this problem with clear vision:

> The politics is hard. There is massive pressure from business not to act
> … Look around the world and you see many examples of competition
> bodies that succumbed to these pressures.[11]

Ignoring this effect is akin to declaring deregulation a success after the initial burst of entry. Claiming that 'politics ruins good policy' is tautological. The appropriate course of action is to acknowledge the reality of politics and to determine what can be done about it.

The most immediate policy implication is that deregulation should not be attempted if it will not attain a sufficient degree of competition initially. Any initial success less than this is only an illusion.

Policy Implication #1: If the industry structure is such that market competition will not be sufficiently intense, deregulation imposes a deadweight loss on society and should not be undertaken.

The free market is not a saviour. It is often argued that competition in the marketplace will improve upon a regulated structure. This is a false choice. Competition certainly arises following deregulation, but it is not competition for customers. Instead, it is competition over monopoly rents. And that need not leave society better off. Reform efforts, therefore, are more productively spent looking for better ways to make deregulation work or better ways to regulate an industry.

The threshold of 'sufficiently intense' is, of course, imprecise. The analysis above has shown how the threshold can be calculated in a simple model.

---

11   Quoted in Kelly (2009, p. 150).

Critically, the threshold is not set in stone. It is a function of the market structure, its costs and its benefits, as well as the nature of the political environment. If lobbying costs go up, takeovers are more expensive, and market competition is 'stickier'. If the speed of takeovers slows down (lower m), the profitability of takeovers also goes down and market competition persists. Many other institutional variables beyond these explicit model parameters carry similar implications. All of these actions, by affecting outcomes post-deregulation, feed back into the logic of the decision to deregulate.

Policy Implication #2: Deregulation is a better policy if lobbying is more expensive (L is larger) or bureaucratic approval of takeovers is slower and sequential (m is lower).

The design variables that improve deregulation are, effectively, changes that throw sand in the gears of policy making. The lobbying cost can be increased by allowing the government official to set his/her own price and keep some of the revenue.

The cost of lobbying can also be increased by bureaucratic inefficiency. By making it more difficult, and thus more costly, to get a takeover approved, firms are less likely to attempt them. This implication runs counter to our usual intuitions. It says that a deliberately inefficient bureaucratic system may perversely make some policies work better. A curse of the Australian system may be its technocratic efficiency (efficiency has other upsides, to be sure). This insight accords with classic theories of bureaucratic structure that it is inefficient not by accident but by design. Moe (1989, p. 267) argues that 'American public bureaucracy is not designed to be effective. The bureaucracy arises out of politics, and its design reflects the interests, strategies, and compromises of those who exercise political power.' The literature that Moe is a part of sees the inefficient design as serving the interests of the bureaucrats themselves, or the self-interest of their political masters. Our insight is that this inefficiency may serve the interests of the political masters, not for self-interested reasons but rather for the interests of society. No country desires a chaotic bureaucratic system, to be sure, but the general lesson is that speed may in some circumstances be a curse rather than a virtue, and that this can be controlled without necessarily making the bureaucracy chaotic.

Many tools and mechanisms beyond those in the model can be leveraged to serve the same ends. For instance, in the model, takeovers are made by a single predatory firm that is selected by nature at the beginning of play. This sets up the predator to engage in far-sighted behaviour. When takeovers are constrained, the initial takeovers it engages in are typically unprofitable. It is possible that all takeovers are unprofitable up until the final one. The predator nevertheless pursues them as, looking down the game-tree, it sees the prize of monopoly control at the end. To the extent that this belief can be shaken, that it is uncertain which firm will attain the prize of monopoly, the willingness to engage in the early, unprofitable takeovers will be undermined. Without these takeovers, of course, monopoly can't be attained, and competition post-deregulation is stickier. The lesson from this discussion is that the sequence of takeovers, the sequence by which market concentration is attained, matters for the final outcome, and matters for the efficacy of deregulation itself.

A similar conclusion follows if we allow imperfect spillover of the gains from a takeover. In the model, we consider the extreme case in which a take-over does not deliver to the predator any market dominance. All remaining firms benefit identically and the subsequent equilibrium remains symmetric, albeit with fewer firms competing. In practice, that spillover is likely to be imperfect, and the predator will capture more of the benefit of the decrease in competition. In turn, this makes takeovers more profitable and increases the competitive threshold at which deregulation will unwind. A counter to that is for policy makers to not allow a single firm to roll-up the entire industry. The impact of a takeover matters not just by what is lost but who gains. An implication is that more balanced market concentration – by which the market would move from competition to monopoly – may make concentration less appealing and, therefore, deregulation work better.[12]

Indices such as the Hirschman–Herfindahl index have long emphasised the relative size of firms over concentration indices that lump some of the largest firms together. What our discussion adds is that this difference matters when traced back to the deregulatory decision itself, and that to make deregulation work better, policy makers can focus on the sequence in which takeovers occur and the identity of the firms that undertake them. As this point is beyond the specification of the model and, thus, we can only sketch the intuition here, we state this policy implication in a generic and surely understated way.

Policy Implication #3: The sequence of takeovers matters for the effective-ness of deregulation. A more balanced path of market concentration is likely to increase the efficacy of deregulation.

---

12   The degree of spillover surely varies by industry. This discussion adds another dimension to how policy makers can identify the circumstances in which deregulation is likely to unwind and in which circumstances it creates competition that is likely to stick.

In addition to implications for the market participants, we can also draw out implications for their political masters. In an ideal world, policy makers would all be benevolent with the interests of society at heart. In practice, policy makers are human and subject to self-interest. The perspective we take here is that this is a given but that the ability of policy makers to extract rents and distort outcomes is dependent on the structure of the political institutions and the incentives it gives rise to.

In the context of deregulatory programs, one key institutional design choice is which policy maker gets to make which decisions. Two distinct sets of decisions are present: the decision to deregulate in the first place and the decisions to approve takeovers. Even if all policy makers are equally self-interested, separating these decisions improves outcomes. In particular, if the policy makers who make the decision to deregulate are not also the policy makers who are lobbied to approve takeovers, then they will not incorporate the rents from lobbying into their decision to deregulate. These policy makers will then have a clear view of deregulation, and, if they anticipate that the initial burst of competition will only be unwound, they will not deregulate.

Policy Implication #4: Separating the political decision to deregulate from the approval of takeovers can avoid inefficient cycles of firm entry and exit and deregulatory failures.

This institutional design feature does not get us to a first best outcome, but it can avoid destructive cycles. It can avoid the adoption of policies for which failure is inevitable. A self-interested policy maker who controls both sets of decisions will anticipate future lobbying rents and so be tempted to adopt a policy not despite its likely failure, but precisely because its failure is inevitable.[13]

The Australian electricity industry

Any retrospective assessment on the Australian electricity reform that was begun in the 1990s would see two key failures: first, that deregulation is incomplete, with state governments, particularly in Queensland, moving slowly to deregulate their markets; second, there is the absence of a deep and stable market for electricity. The first failure is clearly political, as state

---

13   The historical failures of deregulatory policies may also be attributed to error. Policy makers have deregulated more on hope than reality. The arguments presented here will help avoid future errors of this nature, but only if the policy makers themselves don't benefit from that failure.

governments have been reluctant to expose sensitive markets (in particular in rural Queensland) to the vicissitudes of market competition.

The second failure, whilst nominally a market-based failure, is also, at base, a political failure. The electricity generation industry is marked by a large entry cost – full-scale power plants – and a smaller number of firms that can be supported, leading to a more consolidated industry.[14] This contrasts with the retail business with small entry costs and potentially many more firms competing. The reforms of the 1990s deregulated both ends of the industry, generation and retail, and treated them separately and similarly. The ideas described in this chapter show how, when politics is added to the analysis, the difference in entry cost can be a key predictor of market evolution post-deregulation. It shows that industries with large entry costs will backslide, and that early bursts of competition are only illusory. That is the pattern that played out in Australia.

The core of the political failure was allowing the industry to consolidate.[15] This implies that when we back up to the decision to deregulate power generation, we see that as constituting a policy failure as well. If consolidation is predictable, then deregulation is a mistake. The process could have been improved significantly if the core political problem could have been identified and addressed and the recommendations of the previous section factored into the analysis.

The failure in deregulation policy extends beyond generation. Although the retail segment of the industry is marked by low costs and entry was extensive – and almost surely sufficient to exceed the threshold for maintaining competition within that market – in allowing vertical integration, policy makers set that segment of the market on a path of increasing consolidation as well. This is a clear demonstration of the difficulty in politicians holding back the tide of market power and only approving good mergers. Vertical integration often enhances efficiency, an argument that was easy to make in this industry, in part because of the emerging difficulties in the spot market that were exacerbated by the mergers themselves. Allowing crossover between generation and retail has, however, only set the market on a path in which deregulation fails at both ends of the value chain.

---

14   Efficiency returns in operating multiple power plants implies that the number of firms that can be supported is less than the number of plants necessary to supply the Australian market.

15   The extent to which the ACCC opposed and fought the mergers is unclear. In the event that the ACCC's opposition was in fact strident, that it lacked the power and tools to stop the mergers is then a political failure at the legislative level.

Nevertheless, we are where we are. What should come next in reform of the Australian electricity industry? The lessons of this chapter do not leave one hopeful that meaningful reform could be achieved that limits the power of the largest players in generation. A first step would be to separate generation from retail and break up the gen-tailers. They will surely push back, arguing that vertical integration allows them to provide a better service. But it must be acknowledged that this benefit comes at a large cost.[16]

If policy makers are not prepared to break up the gen-tailers, they must acknowledge that market competition in generation is off the table and consider more direct forms of control. This could take the form of price caps that electricity cannot exceed; it could involve more and closer government scrutiny of company decisions, particularly decisions to shut down power plants that significantly choke supply to the retail market. If open market competition cannot take hold, then more centralised control tools are warranted.

The opportunity of renewable energy

The free variable in all of this is the rise of renewable energy. It is here where policy action on competition will have the most lasting impact. Through the frame of this chapter, the issue will be the cost of entry into the renewable space and the number of new entrants that build capacity and enter the market. While solar generation began with rooftop solar, the age of utility-scale solar projects is already upon us. This will lead to the emergence of large solar players, yet the scale of solar farms is relatively small compared to the typical coal-fired (or gas-fired) plant that they will replace. The largest solar farm today is the 649MW facility in Tamil Nadu, India. In contrast, the Eraring coal-fired plant in NSW owned by Origin Energy and slated to be closed in 2032 generates 2880MW of power.

The smaller scale of project implies a lower entry cost for renewables and a generation market that can sustain much more competition. Closer empirical work is necessary to confirm that this level is beyond the threshold identified in our model. If it is, the transition to clean energy will not only bring environmental benefits to Australia but it may also solve the market competition problem that followed deregulation.

Key policy choices will be made and these must be decided with the goal of achieving a robust level of competition. The gen-tailers' strategy will surely

---

16   The federal government's 'big stick' policy proposal threatens actions along these lines although the intent to carry them out is unclear. https://www.smh.com. au/politics/federal/big-stick-laws-need-major-rewrite-to-avoid-consumer-pain-says-energy-sector-20191006-p52y21.html.

be to use their current position of market dominance to transition to the same position in the market for renewable energy. The Australian Government must prevent this from happening. A simple extrapolation from the model reported here shows that while a market with a significant level of competition could be stable and robust to political forces, it is simultaneously true that a more concentrated market will also be stable and, should concentration take hold initially, movement from there to a more competitive situation is difficult if not impossible.

This delivers two key policy recommendations. First, should new market entry occur, the government must not allow consolidation, particularly from the existing dominant firms. This action will surely generate political pressure and economic arguments about efficiency. Both must be resisted. Second, the government would be well served making it *more* difficult for the gen-tailers to move into renewable energy. This may sound counter-intuitive – that restraining competition may actually improve competition. It is not a general lesson, to be sure, but completely open markets don't always (or even often) work well, and this has been evident in energy. By restraining the ability of the gen-tailers to move their dominance to the new sector, the government will provide the conditions for a more truly competitive market to flourish.

If this opportunity is wasted, it will be difficult if not impossible to recreate. The new technology of solar and wind energy offers the promise of many benefits to society. An additional, less appreciated, benefit is that it might also provide the opportunity to fix Australia's broken energy markets.

5.   Concluding discussion

The objective of this chapter is to change the lens through which economic reform is viewed. Economic theory has advanced enormously in the last half century, particularly the theory of industrial organisation that studies market competition and the behaviour of firms. These theories have provided the basis for competition policy in Australia and around the world and have set that policy on a much sounder footing. The problem is that no matter how precise this theory is, in practice it runs into politics. That politics matters is not a new point. Indeed, in the 2004 report of the Australian Government's Productivity Commission (p. 172), the Commission argued that 'mechanisms that can help to lock in the gains of previous competition related and other reforms should be a central component of the procedural framework attaching to any future reform agenda'.

The Commission clearly sees the problem of making reforms stick. But in its report, and all surrounding discussion, there is not a model of why backsliding occurs and how it varies by industry structure. Without a model of how the political and market environments interact, policy makers attempting to solve the problem are doing little more than guessing. The effort of this chapter is to put some meat on those bones and provide a theory – and a prediction – for when backsliding is likely to occur. With a theoretical foundation for the phenomenon, policy makers can then begin to understand what policy levers will work and begin to implement them.

If anything, the analysis herein *understates* the impact that politics has on market outcomes. We have focused on how market consolidation allows large firms to exercise power over markets. It is increasingly apparent that the power of large firms extends also to politics. If market power enables political power and vice versa in a reinforcing cycle, then backsliding from competition in markets will lead to even worse outcomes in politics that will end with a small number of players having a stranglehold on market and political outcomes.[17] In a recent book, Wu (2018) argues that the dominance of large firms threatens a subversion of democracy itself. Although Australia is not at the same precipice as is the United States and other countries, the signs are concerning. Indeed, in the electricity market, prices for retail customers have fluctuated and increased due to the actions of large firms to reduce supply by closing early large generation plants. In natural gas, the signing of several large overseas contracts has threatened the very supply of gas to the domestic market and caused direct intervention of the Prime Minister.[18] Similar exercising of market power is evident in banking and other industries.

Market power limits the ability of politicians to control competition. This effect is easy to see with self-interested policy makers as the rents are larger when the market is dominated by large players with both more profit to play with and more to gain from advantageous government policy. It is less easy to see but no less important when policy makers are public-spirited. In that case, large market players have an even larger threat to hold over policy makers as, by restraining supply, they can hurt consumers and not only withhold

---

17   Although see Callander, Foarta, and Sugaya (2022b) for a model of this feedback
      loop and an argument for why the feedback loop between market and political
      power may be bounded.

18   'Gas export controls on hold as government strikes deal with suppliers',
      ABC News, 26 September 2017, https://www.abc.net.au/news/2017-09-27/
      gas-export-controls-on-hold-amid-government-agreement/8993254.

payment of rents to the policy makers. Regardless of the motivations of individuals, all policy makers in a democracy require re-election, and the power over the public held by large firms – and the frequent inability of voters to assign blame – gives those firms substantial political power. One need only look at the political impact of power blackouts recently in South Australia and in the deregulatory experience in California that led to the recall of the Governor, Gray Davis, and the election of Arnold Schwarzenegger. In the above quote from the Australian Government's Productivity Commission, the immediately preceding sentence states that: 'Moreover, backsliding would send an unfortunate signal about the commitment of governments to resisting *pressure from sectional interest groups*' (italics added). If this is the reality, then it must be factored into decisions about market concentration, decisions that heretofore have been made exclusively on economic grounds.

We have focused on deregulation in industries that began as natural monopolies, such as that for electricity in Australia and around the world. The model, and the underlying ideas, are broadly applicable to deregulatory policies. In industries with many firms and some degree of competition before deregulation, the announcement of deregulation has led to merger waves as the incumbent firms prepare for the coming freedom and attendant lobbying opportunities.[19] Whether mergers and market consolidation occurs after or before deregulation is implemented, the same self-interested behaviour is unleashed. Adam Smith instructed us to admire this in markets but subsequent experience has taught us to be wary, and to see the need to harness self-interest for the greater good. This chapter is an attempt to do the same in politics: to acknowledge self-interested behaviour and to begin to understand how it can be channelled for the greater good. The analysis we report here shows that this pursuit is useful not only for the sake of politics, but for the analysis and design of markets as well.

---

19   This dynamic has been evident even in the electricity industry. In Sweden, for instance, the regional electricity companies engaged in a series of mergers prior to deregulation in order for the larger combined companies to better compete both in the market and in the political domain. See Högselius and Kaijser (2010) for a detailed account.

References

Australian Energy Regulator (2017). 'State of the Energy Market 2017'. Retrieved from https://www.aer.gov.au/publications/state-of-the-energy-market-reports/state-of-the-energy-market-2017.

Callander, Steven, Dana Foarta, and Takuo Sugaya (2022). 'The Conditional Nature of Policy Outcomes: Market Response and Policy Impact over Time'. Working paper, Stanford University.

Callander, Steven, Dana Foarta, and Takuo Sugaya (2022b). 'Market Competition and Political Influence: An Integrated Approach'. Working paper, Stanford University.

Fox-Penner, Peter (2014). *Smart Power: Climate Change, the Smart Grid, and the Future of Electric Utilities*. Island Press, Washington DC.

Högselius, Per, and Arne Kaijser (2010). 'The Politics of Electricity Deregulation in Sweden: The Art of Acting on Multiple Arenas'. *Energy Policy*, Vol. 38, No. 5: 2245–2254.

Kelly, Paul (2009). *The March of Patriots: The Struggle for Modern Australia*. Melbourne University Press, Melbourne.

Mankiw, N. Gregory, and Michael D. Whinston (1986). 'Free Entry and Social Inefficiency'. *RAND Journal of Economics*, Vol. 17, No. 1 (Spring): 48–58.

Moe, Terry M. (1989). 'The Politics of Bureaucratic Structure'. In *Can the Government Govern?* John E. Chubb and Paul E. Peterson (eds). Brookings Institution, Washington DC.

National Competition Council (2005). 'Assessment of Governments' Progress in Implementing the National Competition Policy and Related Reforms: 2005'. Commonwealth of Australia (October).

Philippon, Thomas (2019). *The Great Reversal: How America Gave Up on Free Markets*. Harvard University Press, Cambridge.

Posner, Richard A. (1975). 'The Social Costs of Monopoly and Regulation'. *Journal of Political Economy*, Vol. 83, No. 4 (August): 807–828.

Salant, Stephen W., Sheldon Switzer, and Robert J. Reynolds (1983). 'Losses From Horizontal Merger: The Effects of an Exogenous Change in Industry Structure on Cournot–Nash Equilibrium'. *Quarterly Journal of Economics*, Vol. 98, No. 2 (May): 185–199.

Wu, Tim (2018). *The Curse of Bigness: Antitrust in the New Gilded Age*. Columbia Global Reports, New York.

Chapter 4

Prospects for Battery Investment under More Spatially Granular Electricity Spot Pricing

Orrie Johan, Gordon Leslie, Tom Meares
and Russell Pendlebury[1]

1. Introduction

The clean energy transition will see increased shares of electricity generation from zero-carbon, intermittent resources, and lower shares from more emissions-intensive, dispatchable, fossil-fuel resources. In Australia's National Electricity Market (NEM), this is already being observed, with total output shares for grid-scale wind and solar electricity generators increasing from 2% in 2010 to 14% in 2020, and output shares for coal and gas resources falling from 90% to 78% over that same period.[2] This continued penetration of intermittent resources will result in modern electricity grids and markets that differ significantly to those that existed when contestable wholesale electricity markets were introduced during the initial wave of electricity sector restructuring in the late 1990s and early 2000s.

This chapter is motivated by three areas of change that electricity sectors will experience when undergoing a clean energy transition.

---

1   **Orrie Johan**, **Tom Meares** and **Russell Pendlebury**, Australian Energy Market Commission; **Gordon Leslie**, Department of Economics, Monash University.
     The views and opinions expressed in this article are those of the authors and do not necessarily reflect those of the Australian Energy Market Commission or Monash University.
2   Author calculations using the AEMO MMS database.

- First, the deployment and operation of storage assets and flexible load assets. These assets are not widely deployed in today's major markets, but the value of these assets increases with the increasing penetration of intermittent generating sources insofar as wholesale prices exhibit greater hour-to-hour volatility. For example, storage or flexible load assets can buy and use cheap energy when the sun is shining and the wind is blowing, but then dispatch energy (or reduce energy use) during dark and still conditions.
- Second, the transmission network and location of generators. Rather than having a network that is centred around delivering electricity generated by large power stations near fossil-fuel resources to population and industry centres, the network will be more decentralised to service areas with suitable wind and solar resources for electricity generation.
- Finally, market designs for wholesale electricity. Electricity market rules that were implemented in the 1990s might be less suitable for delivering efficient operating and investment signals in more decentralised networks with more intermittent technology mixes associated with the clean energy transition.

This chapter examines how the prospects for battery investment and operation are likely to be impacted by market reforms that introduce more spatially granular spot pricing of electricity. This links two active developments in the NEM: (1) the introduction of grid-scale batteries, and (2) the proposed market design reforms that seek to introduce *locational marginal pricing*, partially in response to the changing nature of transmission congestion in periods with high levels of output from renewable resources.[3]

The NEM, like most electricity markets around the world, has a *zonal* wholesale electricity market design, characterised by having large administrator-defined uniform-price regions. *Nodal* market designs, as seen in the USA, New Zealand and Singapore, are characterised by having *locational marginal prices* (LMPs), which were first developed in Bohn, Caramanis and Schweppe (1984). Nodal prices differ from zonal prices by incorporating the congestion externality (if any) from injecting/withdrawing energy at the specific network location. A growing literature emphasises the challenges associated with zonal

---

3   Refer to Australian Energy Market Commission (2020) for an outline of the reform proposals and motivations. Further work on these reforms is currently being progressed by the Energy Security Board as part of post-2025 electricity market design work, in the Transmission and Access workstream.

market designs and the strengths of nodal market designs in the context of the renewable energy transition (e.g. see Cramton 2017; Wolak 2019; Katzen and Leslie 2020; Graf et al. 2020).

The analysis in this chapter proceeds in two parts. First, we discuss some revenue components that enter the business case for battery storage in the context of Australia's zonal market design, before emphasising how this case changes under the nodal pricing reform proposed for the NEM. By virtue of having more price series available with locational marginal prices, there should be more profitable opportunities for batteries under a nodal market design. We present indicative evidence that the extra profits available to batteries under a nodal market design could be large and economically meaningful because the pricing methodology allows batteries to receive greater compensation when they site in areas where they can relieve transmission congestion. We then contrast these results with the business models for the first batteries deployed in Australia and note that they (a) are not yet primarily used for energy arbitrage, (b) are all owned and operated by entities that have other generating, network or retailing interests in the NEM, and (c) have all been deployed with some form of public funding support.

The second part documents some features of the battery rollout observed in California, USA, following their Forward Battery Build Program (California Public Utilities Commission (CPUC) 2020). California adopted locational marginal prices in 2009, and has a larger stock of existing and proposed batteries than Australia and the other US regions. We show that batteries in California, like those in Australia, tend to site in areas with relatively higher energy arbitrage opportunities, but energy arbitrage is not the primary use for the majority of the batteries. Taken together, the analysis of battery deployment in Australia and California suggests that energy arbitrage has not been the key driver of battery viability to date in either market. However, Australia appears to have much greater heterogeneity in the value of energy arbitrage across different transmission network locations, suggesting that adopting a nodal market design should improve future business cases for batteries in the NEM. We conclude by offering areas for further research relating to market reforms tied to clean energy transitions and their relevance to storage and flexible load technologies.

2. Batteries and wholesale electricity pricing in Australia's National Electricity Market (NEM)

The recent history of large-scale battery deployment in Australia's NEM is one of rapidly declining costs, increasing interest in the technology and a few landmark early developments. However, the scale of projects built to date in Australia is small relative to the penetration of intermittent renewable generation.

The investment and operational case for a battery is derived from several spot markets, contract markets, or privately contracted arrangements. Some of the most notable options for grid-scale battery revenue observed or being considered today (US Energy Information Administration (EIA) 2020) are:

- Providing system services, such as frequency regulation, voltage support or reactive power support;
- Co-located firming of generators such as wind or solar farms;
- Transmission and distribution investment deferral by managing the load on the transmission or distribution level below its specified maximum level;
- Arbitrage in the wholesale market for energy, where batteries charge using inexpensive electrical energy and discharge when prices for electricity are high. This option allows large-scale batteries to alleviate congestion on the transmission network (just as they would for transmission deferral) but does so through responses to spot price incentives.

The analysis in this chapter focuses on grid-scale batteries; however, we briefly note some additional revenue streams that have been documented for behind-the-meter batteries (University of Queensland 2020):

- Peak demand lopping for significant loads that face peak demand network charges;[4] and
- Providing virtual cap products for significant loads that would otherwise purchase these products directly or indirectly from the contract market.

Batteries can be more rapidly deployed than traditional firming capacity and in many contexts are more flexible in terms of where they can locate (Fluence 2019; Kirkpatrick 2020). The deployment of batteries would appear to benefit from specific price information in relation to where they should or should not be located. When compared to the regional prices inherent to zonal markets, the locational marginal prices (LMPs) inherent to nodal markets provide batteries with more granular price distributions at specific points on the network as a consequence of the interaction of:

---

4   Operators of large loads can be motivated to shave their peak demand if they face a peak demand charge in their downstream network or retail pricing. We do not investigate or discuss the efficiency of such tariffs in this chapter.

- Concentrations of generation, in particular intermittent generation;
- Concentrations of load; and
- Constraints on the transmission network.[5]

Specifically, in the context of the NEM, the bids that market participants submit to express their willingness to inject or withdraw electricity are converted to a series of shadow locational marginal prices at every network node. These shadow LMPs represent the marginal as-bid value to all market participants (generators and end-users) for an incremental injection or withdrawal of energy at a given network node. In a nodal market design, these are the prices that market participants face. In the zonal NEM, all market participants face the shadow LMP calculated at their *regional reference node* (RRN), known as the *regional reference price* (RRP).[6] An identity defined by the Australian Energy Market Operator (AEMO) that links these prices is:

$$LMP_i = RRP_i - MPA_i$$

where i denotes the network node, and MPA_i is the mis-pricing adjustment at node i that must occur in order for each market participant to face the same regional price. This identity makes clear the potential for situations where the economic value of additional generation at two locations differs (their LMPs differ), but where equal amounts of generation at each location receive the same compensation (they settle at the same RRP). As stated by the AEMO, 'the disjoint between the local prices [LMPs] caused by network congestion and the RRPs used for settlement can ... discourage economic efficiency' (AEMO 2019).

The locations and sizes of generation resources, transmission capacity and load across the network, and the extent to which the power system is transitioning toward higher shares of intermittent resources that are located away from load centres, have a direct bearing on future distributions and the economic importance of location specific prices. Batteries, perhaps more than any other technology, would seem to value more granular price signals for whether to invest, where to invest and how to operate. A single regional reference price by comparison delivers less information to investors about where and when to invest in battery technology. Battery investors weighing an energy arbitrage business model in the NEM have five price series to consider under the existing

---

5   There are also relevant non-transmission constraints included in the dispatch engine that can impact locational prices. See Katzen and Leslie (2020) for a further discussion.

6   The RRN is approximately located in the load-centre for each NEM region, which are defined by state borders.

market design, but would have many hundreds of LMP series to consider under a nodal market design. They should be able to find a more profitable price series (or at least as good) as the RRP price series for energy arbitrage among the many LMP series.[7]

Profit-seeking energy arbitrageurs in a nodal market improve the efficiency of the network and help in achieving least-cost supply outcomes for end-users. By definition, the location with the biggest LMP price spreads provides the biggest difference in value to the system of relieving congestion when charging (perhaps when sited next to wind and solar farms away from a load centre), and discharging when demand is high and lines are relatively free of congestion (perhaps in the evening peak when the sun has set).[8] Therefore, nodal market designs better align the incentives of battery operators and investors with the goals of policy makers and customers.[9] The information and incentives provided by LMPs are particularly useful during periods of rapid growth in renewable technology deployment, where a significant amount of renewable capacity may have been added in parts of the network with limited transmission capacity (Falvi 2020).

Profit-seeking energy arbitrageurs in zonal markets have a less clear impact on economic efficiency because the prices they face depart from the marginal economic value of their actions when the network is congested. Where a battery acts to relieve a network constraint in such a market, it pays or receives the same revenues as a battery that charges/discharges the same amount of energy anywhere in that region, regardless of the impact the other battery has on network constraints, and hence the lowest cost combination of generation to meet load. Therefore, efficiency-improving actions by batteries are under-compensated

---

7   The current zonal price, the RRP, is the LMP at the Regional Reference Node (RRN). Therefore the LMP at the RRN will still exist in the NEM under a nodal market design.

8   Prices and marginal economic value align under the framework of Bohn, Caramanis and Schweppe (1984) where generating resources are offered at marginal cost. In practice, firms may have the ability to exercise market power. Refer to Harvey and Hogan (2000) for a discussion of the properties of nodal markets and zonal markets in the presence of market power, and Potomac Economics (2019) and The Brattle Group (2018) for a discussion of market power mitigation mechanisms for nodal market designs.

9   This price signal helps indicate the best place to deploy battery technology to improve the efficiency of the electricity market and could potentially defer or remove the need for expansion of the transmission network by helping to alleviate constraints at particular times of the day (CAISO 2019; Leslie et al. 2020). Indeed, some studies claim that network expansion deferral will provide the greatest welfare benefits from storage deployment (Go et al. 2016; Mallapragada et al. 2020).

when they alleviate congestion under zonal market designs (Katzen and Leslie 2020), with a further consequence being that entrants might not be incentivised to site at the best location from a network perspective.

Figure 1: Average daily demand and price profiles, South Australia

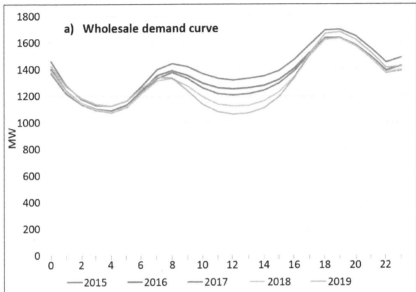

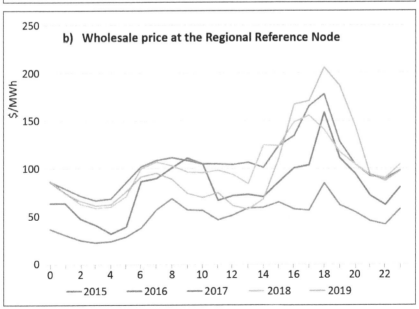

Notes: X-axis is hour-of-day, with lines plotting averages by half-hour-of-day.
Source: Author calculations using the AEMO Market Management System (MMS) Database.

In the next section, we compare the energy arbitrage opportunities available in the NEM under the existing zonal market design with those that are available if they could access the existing shadow locational marginal prices. Batteries in the NEM have to date been deployed under business cases that attach greater emphasis to frequency control ancillary services (FCAS) market revenues than energy arbitrage revenues to recoup their investment costs (Aurecon 2018, 2019). However, with FCAS revenues being relatively small when compared to energy revenues for the whole market, it is likely that energy arbitrage will become a crucial component for many battery business cases at some point in the future. For example, the classic solar 'duck curve', as seen in Figure 1a and 1b (previous page) for South Australia, is shown to result in additional solar installations pushing down daytime system load and prices, and pushing up evening prices, thereby improving the value of within-day energy arbitrage.[10] Indeed, some battery storage owners have indicated that arbitrage may become an increasingly important portion of their battery's overall revenue stream, relative to the revenue derived from providing FCAS services (University of Queensland 2020).

Price signals for battery investment and operation in the NEM today (in $/MWh)

Figure 2 displays the average intra-day price variation in the five regions of the NEM between the highest priced two hours in the trading day and the two lowest prices. In other words, with perfect foresight over the course of 2019, this is the revenue in $/MWh that a 2-hour duration battery with 100% charge/discharge efficiency and no loss factor adjustment could have derived from the market in each region per day. This is a simplified measure used to assess the energy arbitrage opportunities for a small battery, similar in nature to those used in Graves, Jenkins and Murphy (1999), Bathurst and Strbac (2003), Jenkin and Weiss (2005), Figueiredo, Flynn and Cabral (2006), Hessami and Bowly (2011) and Staffell and Rustomji (2016).

There are a number of things to note about this. First, there are only five signals. Second, there is a significant difference between the signal in some regions compared to others. The magnitude of the arbitrage signal in South Australia is more than double that in Queensland. As was noted in the prior section, wholesale arbitrage is not the only market a battery will have recourse to in justifying its business case. However, this wide disparity reflects the importance of even coarse locational signals in finding a location in the NEM with strong wholesale price arbitrage opportunities for battery deployment.

---

10   This phenomenon is also documented in California (Bushnell and Novan 2018) and Western Australia (Jha and Leslie 2019).

Figure 2: Average intra-day price spread at the Regional Reference Nodes, 2019

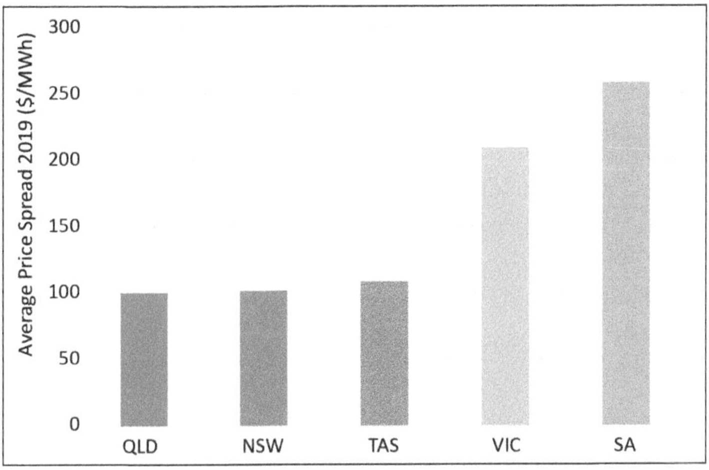

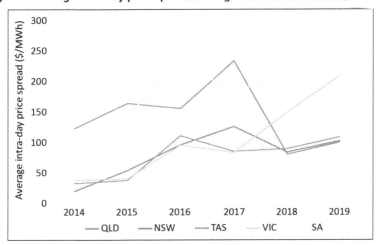

Notes: Average daily intra-day price variation. Highest consecutive two-hour period compared to the lowest consecutive two-hour period, based on 5-minute dispatch data.
Source: Author calculations using the AEMO MMS Database.

Figure 3 informs the degree to which this arbitrage signal changes from year to year. The signal in each region has varied significantly with an upward trajectory, with South Australia (which contains the highest levels of generation shares by intermittent resources) being in the top two regions for wholesale price arbitrage opportunities in each of the past five years.

Figure 3: Average intra-day price spreads at Regional Reference Nodes, 2014–19

Notes: Average daily intra-day price variation. Highest consecutive two-hour period compared to the lowest consecutive two-hour period, based on 5-minute dispatch data.
Source: Author calculations, NEM Regional Reference Price data, 2014–2019.

Price signals in the NEM under shadow locational marginal prices (in $/MWh)

While the NEM currently settles at regional references prices, AEMO's dispatch engine also calculates shadow locational marginal prices for all trading intervals. These prices differ from the regional reference price by adding or subtracting the value additional generation at each location has on network congestion.[11] However, there is a caveat: the shadow LMPs in this analysis are not the prices that market participants are currently subject to. Therefore, the price distribution of LMPs under a nodal market design may differ from the shadow LMPs under a zonal market design due to different participant incentives (Katzen and Leslie 2020). However, this exercise will still provide insight into the significance of the statistical argument that having many more price series for batteries to choose from when siting in a congested network should provide better energy arbitrage opportunities. With LMPs, new entrants would have many hundreds of price series to choose from when siting, compared with the current five on offer under the NEM's existing market design.[12]

Using these prices, we display the average arbitrage spreads for each shadow locational marginal price in the NEM for 2019 in Figure 4, with each of the five regional reference nodes highlighted.

There are three things to note. First, there are many more locational marginal prices or price points to inform the case for additional battery investment across the NEM. Second, there is substantial heterogeneity within each NEM region, and most regions appear to have some nodes at the higher end of the overall arbitrage signal spectrum. This is summarised in Table 1, which presents the difference in the highest and lowest nodes in terms of average intra-day price spread over 2019. For example, in New South Wales, the location with the highest average shadow LMP spread was $178 higher than the RRP price spread. The difference between the highest shadow LMP price spread and the RRP price spread would represent

---

11   See Bohn, Caramanis and Schweppe (1984) for the derivation of locational marginal prices. The shadow LMPs used in this analysis are equal to the as-bid whole of system cost from withdrawing 1MWh of energy at the specified node. Refer to AEMO (2019) for the derivation of these prices in the context of the NEM, and Katzen and Leslie (2020) for further discussion on the interpretation of shadow LMPs obtained from a zonal market context.

12   There is a second caveat that we do not explore: the prices we study ignore transmission loss factors. These factors are easily incorporated into locational marginal prices (see Bohn et al., 1984), but are not dynamically calculated and applied in the NEM under the existing market rules, and are therefore unavailable for our study.

a major change in the business case for storage if this price distribution was available to a new entrant. Third and finally, the existing batteries in the NEM (described in the section below, 'The build-out of utility-scale batteries to date in the NEM') are sited in areas with greater price spreads when considering the whole NEM, but not all are at locations within their regions with the greatest price spreads.

Figure 4: Average intra-day price spread for all nodes, 2019

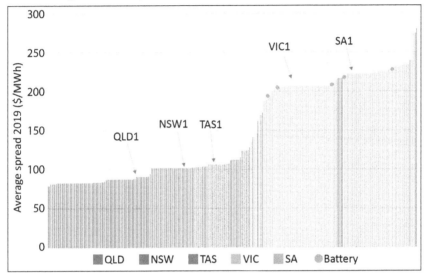

Notes: Average daily intra-day price variation. Highest consecutive two-hour period compared to the lowest consecutive two-hour period, based on 5-minute dispatch data. Prices at the market price floor of –$1000/MWh are removed.
Green dots signify the location of existing batteries in the NEM.
Source: Author calculations, based on the AEMO MMS database, 2019

Table 1: Summary of average price spreads by NEM region

Region	Average Price Spread Low	Average Price Spread RRN	Average Price Spread High	Difference Between High & Low	Difference Between High & RRN
NSW	95	102	280	185	178
QLD	79	91	91	12	0
SA	199	223	274	75	51
TAS	103	106	170	67	64
VIC	135	207	274	139	67

Source: Author calculations, using the AEMO MMS database, 2019.
Summary of information in Figure 5.

It is not only the average spread over a year that provides the investment signal for battery deployment. Extreme price events, or prices above $300/MWh, can provide clear signals for battery deployment and in particular for competing technologies, such as flexible demand technologies or peaking generators. Using the same data set, Figure 5 displays the count of extreme 5-minute price events for each shadow LMP in the NEM over 2019. Again, the five regional reference nodes are highlighted. Approximately one-third of all locations have more than 1000 price events over $300, and there is some meaningful within-region variability in these figures. The locational diversity in these price events could have a significant impact on the incentives for battery deployment and competing technologies if participants are to face LMPs in the future.

Figure 5: Count of extreme price events by node, 2019

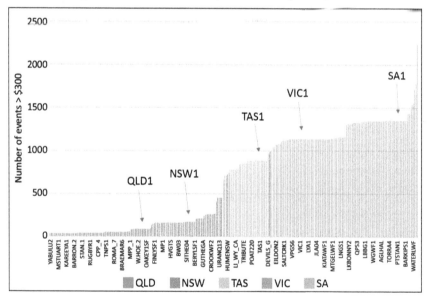

Source: Author calculations, based on the AEMO MMS database, 2019.
Regional reference nodes labelled on the figure.

Summary: Battery deployment and operation under zonal and nodal market designs will differ because the opportunities for within-day energy arbitrage are dependent on market design. Nodal market designs provide many more LMPs for battery investors to consider, and it seems more likely that some of these high price variation nodes will exhibit more persistent price variation signals for battery deployment than those available under a zonal market design. However, we restate the caveat that these price series are not true counterfactuals – the shadow LMPs in this analysis are not the prices that market participants are currently subject to. However, the statistical argument is unchanged: choosing the best price distribution for energy arbitrage will be better with many hundreds of choices under locational marginal pricing than the current five on offer under the NEM's existing market design.

The build-out of utility-scale batteries to date in the NEM

In Australia, large-scale battery storage deployment is still in its early stages. This section first describes some key features of the existing batteries in the NEM, then summarises their characteristics in the context of energy arbitrage and the operating incentives under a zonal versus a nodal market design.

There are currently five registered battery storage systems in excess of 1MW capacity (AEMO 2021). These five systems are:

- Hornsdale Power Reserve in South Australia (100MW/129MWh, operational since 2017);
- Dalrymple North Battery Energy Storage System in South Australia (30MW/8MWh, 2018);
- Ballarat Energy Storage System in Victoria (30MW/30MWh, 2018);
- Gannawarra Energy Storage System in Victoria (25MW/50MWh, 2019); and
- Lake Bonney BESS1[13] in South Australia (25MW/52MWh, 2019).

Hornsdale: The Hornsdale Power Reserve battery in mid-northern South Australia is the first large-scale battery to connect to the NEM and remains the largest. This battery system is owned and operated by Neoen, which has a portfolio of renewable energy assets in the NEM, with the battery co-located with Neoen's Hornsdale Wind Farm.[14] The South Australian Government contributed funding toward the Hornsdale Power Reserve battery's initial development through its Renewable Technology Fund, which was intended to accelerate the uptake of renewable and clean energy technologies in the energy market.[15] The South Australian Government also provided funding for the

---

13   BESS stands for battery energy storage system.

14   See Aurecon (2018) and Neoen (2020).

15   See Department of Treasury and Finance, Government of South Australia (2017), Auditor-General's Department, Government of South Australia (2018), Infigen Energy (2020) and Energy Storage News (2017).

battery's later expansion by 50% through its Grid Scale Storage Fund, which aims to accelerate the rollout of grid-scale energy storage infrastructure and address the intermittency of South Australia's electricity supplies (Department of Energy and Mining South Australia 2019). The Australian Renewable Energy Agency (ARENA) also provided funding for this expansion under its Advancing Renewables Program (ARENA 2019d).

The arrangement with the South Australian Government allows for 30MW/119MWh of the battery's discharge and storage capacity to be used by Neoen for commercial operations, such as FCAS services and price arbitrage in spot markets (ARENA 2019c). The remainder is reserved for power system reliability and other network resilience schemes (AEMO 2018). Another rationale for the battery was noted to be the extended support for the Heywood interconnector by alleviating system security constraints (ElectraNet 2019).

Dalrymple North: The Dalrymple ESCRI-SA (Energy Storage for Commercial Renewable Integration, South Australia) battery on South Australia's Yorke Peninsula is owned by ElectraNet, with some funding provided by ARENA under its Advancing Renewables Program. ElectraNet allocates some battery capacity to provide prescribed transmission services (the Australian Energy Regulator (AER) 2020). A portion of the capital cost is 'ring-fenced' and treated as a capital investment relating to regulated transmission services.[16] The remaining capacity is leased (treated as non-regulated revenue) and operated by AGL so it can use the battery for competitive market services under a lease agreement; AGL is a large participant in the NEM that has both retail operations and generation assets, including wind and gas-fired power stations in South Australia.

The Dalrymple battery focuses on providing reliability in the case of islanding and FCAS to reduce constraints on the Heywood interconnector and improve system security by quickly injecting electricity into the transmission network following a disturbance (ElectraNet 2019).[17]

---

16   See ElectraNet (2018) for more details regarding the capital costs and funding. The regulated transmission services include 'improved connection point reliability in the local network' and fast frequency response.

17   Islanding can occur to a smaller power system (South Australia in this context) when that system needs to continue operating safely and securely after it effectively faces temporary electrical separation from a larger power system (due to some form of transmission failure with Victoria in this context). Refer to WattClarity (2020) for discussion of an islanding case-study.

Ballarat: The Ballarat Energy Storage System is owned by AusNet Services (but does not enter the regulated asset base for this network company) and is operated by EnergyAustralia (AusNet Services 2018). EnergyAustralia is a large participant in the NEM with both retail operations and generation assets, including a coal-fired power station in Victoria. The battery is able to be used commercially for energy arbitrage and FCAS services (EnergyAustralia 2019). As of November 2020, AusNet Services has not used this battery to provide any regulated prescribed transmission services (AER 2020).

The project received public funds that were motivated in large part by locational considerations. It was expected to be able to ease constraints on transmission lines in Western Victoria that reduce the output of wind and solar-generated electricity (ARENA 2019b).[18]

Gannawarra: The Gannawarra Energy Storage System in north-western Victoria is owned by Edify Energy and Wirsol Energy and is operated by EnergyAustralia (Edify Energy 2019). The battery is able to be used commercially for energy arbitrage and FCAS services (EnergyAustralia 2019).

The project received public funds, with one funding body noting its expectation that the battery should be able to ease constraints on transmission lines in western Victoria that will reduce curtailment of output from wind and solar-generated electricity (ARENA 2019a).[19]

Lake Bonney: The Lake Bonney battery in South Australia is owned and operated by Infigen Energy, and is co-located with Infigen's Lake Bonney Wind Farms (Infigen Energy 2020).

---

18   The Victorian Government provided funding for the Ballarat Energy Storage System under the Victorian Energy Storage Initiative, which provided funding for projects to improve the reliability of the Victorian electrical system, drive the development of clean technologies and boost the local economy (Department of Environment, Land, Water and Planning, Government of Victoria, 2020a). ARENA also provided funding for this battery under its Advancing Renewables Program (AusNet Services 2020), which assists projects that can reduce the cost of renewable energy in ways that can increase the value delivered by and the supply of renewable energy in Australia over the long term (ARENA 2020).

19   The Victorian Government provided funding for the Gannawarra Energy Storage System under the Victorian Energy Storage Initiative (Department of Environment, Land, Water and Planning, Government of Victoria, 2020a). ARENA also provided funding under its Advancing Renewables Program (Edify Energy 2019).

The project received public funds, and is being used commercially for energy arbitrage and FCAS services, as well as for firming nearby renewable generation (ibid.).[20]

Summary: These pioneering batteries in the NEM have some common themes: first, each project has received meaningful funding from, or is in partnership with, a government entity; second, there are no independent merchant operators – at least one ownership or operational partner owns nearby renewable resources, owns a major retail operation, or is a network company; third, the batteries owned by network companies have their services ring-fenced, with market-based operations considered as non-regulated revenue and the proportion of capital costs related to those operations not entering the regulated asset base. Finally, at present the majority of battery revenues are not derived from energy arbitrage (Aurecon 2019a).

Budding industries and technologies often receive subsidies that can be economically justified, where the public benefit of developing the technology or supply chain is larger than the private benefit of the first mover. For example, early battery projects may still have costs that exceed the private benefit to the owners or occupiers, but given there can be information spillovers that assist the whole market or future participants, a funding body may determine that a subsidy is appropriate, which may subsequently allow a project to proceed.

Many of the funding bodies cite the benefits each project will have in relieving transmission constraints/renewable curtailment. This could represent another form of spillover that motivates subsidies, where the benefits from the battery are not fully internalised by private investors because other market participants and consumers also benefit from the battery. However, nodal market designs may reduce or eliminate the need for subsidies on congestion relief grounds by better aligning the private investment and operational incentives of storage units with the public benefit of their actions.

Finally, the two batteries with the largest storage capacities are co-located with renewable generating assets that are also owned by the battery owner or operator. Pairing intermittent generators with a flexible asset has obvious

---

20   The South Australian Government provided funding for the Lake Bonney battery through its Renewable Technology Fund. ARENA also provided funding for this battery under its Advancing Renewables Program (Infigen Energy 2020).

appeal. Katzen and Leslie (2020) highlight the competitive advantage battery owners that own renewable assets in the NEM have over independent merchant battery investors due to the zonal market design. A merchant that sites in a location that can relieve congestion affecting local renewables will not receive prices that reflect the value of their congestion-relieving actions. However, the renewable asset that otherwise would have been curtailed will receive a benefit from such actions – they can sell more output to the market. Although a battery owned by a joint-entity does not directly capture their congestion benefit through market prices, the entity as a whole indirectly recovers some portion of the congestion impacts from the battery via their less-curtailed renewable asset that receives the favourable zonal price.

The short-run horizon for large-scale battery storage in Australia

Declining capital expenditure costs are one of the major factors increasing the growth of utility-scale battery storage growth in Australia (ARENA 2017). The costs associated with these devices have plummeted over the past decade, making utility-scale battery deployment increasingly viable across the NEM (Climate Central 2019; Mallapragada et al. 2020; Solar Choice 2014). Coincident with these declining costs are improved revenue opportunities, with Figure 3 presenting an upward trend in potential revenues from energy arbitrage in recent years across the NEM, particularly in South Australia.

A number of additional large-scale battery storage projects are being considered for Australia. In September 2018, the Smart Energy Council outlined five stand-alone large-scale batteries in varying stages of development across the NEM (Smart Energy Council 2018). The Clean Energy Council also recently identified fifteen projects that would mostly be co-located with generation (Clean Energy Council 2018). The large-scale battery storage projects that are expected to be completed in 2021 and 2022 share many of the common themes identified in our earlier discussion of the existing collection of battery assets they would be owned and/or operated by a firm that owns renewable assets in the NEM; receiving public funding; and with multiple major revenue streams outside of market-based energy arbitrage.

One example is Neoen partnering with AusNet Services and Tesla to build the Victorian Big Battery (Premier of Victoria 2020), a 300MW battery in Moorabool, Victoria, that became operational in December 2021 (PV Magazine Australia 2020). The AEMO awarded a System Integrity Protection Scheme contract to Neoen in late 2020 on behalf of the Victorian Government.

Under this contract, AEMO will reserve 250MW of the battery's capacity in summer to operate in this scheme to improve reliability, with claims this will act as 'virtual transmission' in peak demand periods (Department of Environment, Land, Water and Planning, Government of Victoria, 2020b).

As another example, TransGrid has completed the 50MW/75MWh Wallgrove Grid Battery in 2021, located at their Walgrove substation in Western Sydney. This battery will be owned by TransGrid, with dispatch into the wholesale energy market to be operated by Infigen Energy (TransGrid 2020a, 2020b). The battery is expected to commence operations in first quarter 2022, and to provide synthetic inertia and fast frequency response services for the transmission network. The regulatory treatment of this battery is to be confirmed, but could be similar to the Dalrymple North battery, whereby a portion of the capital costs relating to the regulated transmission services enters TransGrid's regulated asset base. The project has received funding from the New South Wales Government's Emerging Energy Program and from ARENA's Advancing Renewables Program (TransGrid 2020b).

Battery energy storage systems (BESSs) as designated 'virtual transmission lines' in Australia

Most of the aforementioned batteries and proposals have predominately been developed to provide system services like FCAS provision, firming renewable energy or peaking services, to provide energy reserves, or to relieve congestion (without entering the regulated asset base of a network company). However, BESS systems are also being contemplated in a regulatory context in Australia to be funded by consumers and obtained by transmission network service providers primarily as an alternative to building additional transmission infrastructure. This concept of BESSs as transmission assets that assist with alleviating congestion, and can only participate in the energy and/or FCAS markets using the non-reserved capacity of the battery, has been referred to as a form of 'virtual transmission'.

Two BESS options were considered as part of the regulatory investment test for transmission on near-term solutions to increase transmission capacity between NSW and Queensland, but neither of these options was pursued further. However, TransGrid and Powerlink as the transmission network service providers in these cases are set to continue to consider virtual transmission options as part of longer-term options for increasing inter-regional capacity between the two states (Powerlink 2019). The AER is currently updating the ring-fencing guidelines for the regulatory treatment of storage devices, which should inform whether batteries as 'virtual transmission' are credible and viable options for future transmission expansions (AER 2020).

Merchant battery investors are likely to be incentivised under nodal market designs to provide similar services to those envisaged in these 'virtual transmission' regulatory settings, since they will be better compensated for constraint-relieving actions. Such market-driven siting and operational decisions would provide a clearer picture of market impacts when evaluating regulatory investment tests for transmission assets, and potentially attenuate the case for batteries to enter the regulated asset base as 'virtual transmission lines'.

3.   Battery deployment in a nodal market: The case of California

California has the greatest penetration of battery assets in the nodal electricity market regions of the United States. In this section we briefly examine the siting decisions of major proposed projects and examine the price spreads associated with energy arbitrage at those locations. Unlike the analysis of the NEM, the locational marginal prices we study in California represent the actual prices faced by market participants at the respective locations.

California has the largest amount of installed utility-scale batteries of any region of the USA (136MW by the end of 2018), and the largest proposed build-out program (California Independent System Operator (CAISO) 2020). California also has a number of policies to incentivise utility-scale batteries, with the build-out still in its relative infancy. The main driver is a 30% tax credit on co-located solar and battery investments, as well as funding provided from the CPUC. Like the NEM, the majority of installed batteries to date in California have received public funds, with energy arbitrage revenue streams much smaller than FCAS revenues (CAISO 2019).

Figure 6 displays the average intra-day price spread for every node in the Californian CAISO market, marking the locations of the 18 proposed batteries that the CPUC consider as 'high confidence' projects.[21] A large proportion of battery build is proposed to be co-located with generation developments such as solar.

Regardless of whether batteries are co-located or standalone, and many of the developments shown in Figure 6 are co-located, it appears that the

---

21   See ftp://ftp.cpuc.ca.gov/energy/modeling/BusbarMapping-Results-
      Battery-2020-03-30.xlsx.

majority of projects in the CPUC's high confidence category to proceed are proposed at locations that currently have above-average intra-day price variation. This may reflect the fact that batteries tend to be co-located with renewable generation developments such as solar, where their intermittency is expected to result in intra-day price variation. However, it may be that energy arbitrage is not the dominant driver of Californian batteries and that these locations have advantageous prospects relating to other contributors to the battery value stack.

Contrasting with our locational price spread analysis of the NEM in Section 2, we observe that although batteries tend to be sited in areas with above-mean price spreads, the average price spreads across locations in CAISO display less heterogeneity than in the NEM, both in terms of the zonal prices and the shadow locational marginal prices. Therefore, the value that batteries can provide in terms of managing congestion appears to be greater in the NEM than in CAISO at present.

Figure 6: Average intra-day price spread for all nodes, CAISO, 2017–2019

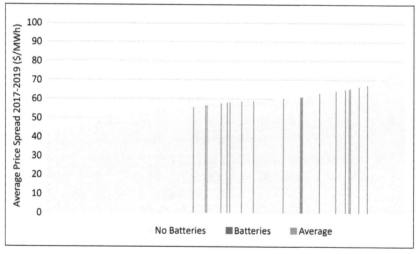

Notes: Average daily intra-day price variation, in $/MWh. Highest hourly period compared to the lowest hourly period. Californian data is hourly. The nodes highlighted as 'Batteries' are the nodes identified in the CPUC mapping as nodes where projects were considered to be 'High Confidence'.
Source: CAISO Open Access Same-time Information System (OASIS), Locational Marginal Prices, 2017–2019.

4. Conclusions and further research

Utility-scale battery deployment is in its infancy, but the value of batteries will increase with greater penetration of intermittent renewable resources in a given network. In particular when the intermittency from renewable penetration provides greater intra-day price spreads, batteries can earn greater revenues via energy arbitrage.

Under nodal market designs, profit-seeking energy arbitrageurs can improve the efficiency of the network and help to achieve least-cost supply outcomes for end-users. This is because they face prices tied to their location in the network that assign value to the congestion impact of their actions. Zonal market designs with uniform-price regions do not provide such a strong link between prices and network efficiency because they do not explicitly reward actions that relieve congestion.

We have found that the value of energy arbitrage has been trending upwards across the five price regions in the NEM, with the highest values observed in renewable-rich South Australia. However, our analysis of shadow locational marginal prices reveals substantial variation in the value that energy arbitrage could provide the transmission network across locations within each region. For example, in New South Wales, we find that the location with the highest average shadow LMP spread was \$178/MWh higher than the observed average zonal price spread.

This suggests that there are certain areas of the network where a battery could provide substantial system benefits, but the current market design does not allow the battery owner to capture the congestion benefits from their actions. We note that the nature of the NEM, with a longer, geographically spread-out network, and with indicative shadow nodal prices that have much wider spreads than observed in California, could well mean that the NEM is likely to benefit from locational signals provided by LMP more than other global electricity markets.

Our examination of the five pioneering batteries in the NEM and the budding developments in California emphasises that there are multiple drivers behind battery business cases, including tax incentive schemes or the provision of services to the grid. It is unclear whether energy arbitrage is a major revenue source for these early deployments. The importance of this driver to a business case will change with increasing amounts of renewable energy deployed in the network. As renewable capacity continues to be added to the NEM, and as more battery capacity is built looking to access FCAS markets, the value of the arbitrage signal and its importance to battery business cases are likely to grow.

This initial analysis of prospects for battery investment under more spatially granular electricity spot pricing has raised several areas for further investigation regarding the economics and regulation of storage and flexible load assets.

First, given the growing interest in considering batteries as a regulated asset to provide 'virtual transmission', further research could investigate: a) the most efficient operating requirements for network companies that seek to use batteries as virtual transmission, and b) the expected siting and operations of batteries that receive market-based compensation under a nodal market design, to c) contrast the economic costs and benefits, along with ratepayer costs and benefits under each model. Nodal market designs may incentivise private battery builds that relieve congestion, and the information content of locational marginal prices may help to defer and/or reinforce the value of proposed large transmission investments.

Relatedly, a second area for further research is motivated by the AER's review of ring-fencing guidelines for the regulatory treatment of storage devices. Batteries can provide market-based and regulated network services. Different ring-fencing regulations and rules for allocations of capital costs into regulated asset bases will impact investment and operation incentives for batteries. Research to inform this review could be of substantial value to many regulators if utility-scale batteries become more commonplace in the coming years and beyond.

Third, the co-locating of batteries and renewables has obvious appeal because the battery can help firm output from the intermittent renewable resource. However, an independent merchant battery owner/operator seeking to site near an existing intermittent resource is at a competitive disadvantage compared to the owner of that intermittent resource under a zonal market design. This warrants further research into the economic significance of this competitive barrier and into the resulting impacts that nodal market designs have on competition in battery deployment and operation.

Finally, our analysis did not examine transmission losses, which are included in the canonical derivation of locational marginal pricing (Bohn et al. 1984). The value of dynamically pricing line losses at each node can be further investigated. It is likely that this again will be advantageous to the business case for batteries, insofar as batteries can be compensated for actions that reduce system losses in addition to relieving congestion.

References

Auditor-General's Department, Government of South Australia (2018, November). Retrieved from https://www.audit.sa.gov.au/LinkClick.aspx?fileticket=4lsqCdK8tgc%3D&tabid=523&portalid=0&mid=1474&forcedownload=true.

Aurecon (2018). *Hornsdale Power Reserve – Year 1 Technical and Market Impact Case Study*. Retrieved from https://www.aurecongroup.com/-/media/files/downloads-library/thought-leadership/aurecon-hornsdale-power-reserve-impact-study-2018.pdf.

Aurecon (2019, September). *Large-Scale Battery Storage Knowledge Sharing Report*. Retrieved from https://arena.gov.au/assets/2019/11/large-scale-battery-storage-knowledge-sharing-report.pdf.

AusNet Services (2018, October). *Ballarat Energy Storage System consortium delivers Victorian Government Energy Storage Initiative ahead of summer*. Retrieved from https://www.ausnetservices.com.au/-/media/Files/AusNet/Media-Releases/Final-2018/Ballarat-Energy-Storage-System-consortium-delivers-Victorian-Government-Energy-Storage-Initiative.ashx.

Australian Energy Market Commission (2020). *Transmission Access Reform: Updated technical specifications and cost–benefit analysis*. Retrieved from https://www.aemc.gov.au/sites/default/files/2020-09/Interim%20report%20-%20transmission%20access%20reform%20-%20Updated%20technical%20specifications%20and%20cost-benefit%20analysis%202020_09_07.PDF.

Australian Energy Market Operator (2018, April). *Initial operation of the Hornsdale Power Reserve Battery Energy Storage System*. Retrieved from https://www.aemo.com.au/-/media/Files/Media_Centre/2018/Initial-operation-of-the-Hornsdale-Power-Reserve.pdf.

Australian Energy Market Operator (2019). Guide to mis-pricing information. Retrieved from https://www.aemo.com.au/-/media/Files/StakeholderConsultation/Consultations/NEM-Consultations/2019/Dispatch/Guide-to-Mis-Pricing-Information.pdf.

Australian Energy Market Operator (2021, January). *NEM Generation information January 2021*. Retrieved from https://acmo.com.au/en/energy-systems/electricity/national-electricity-market-nem/nem-forecasting-and-planning/forecasting-and-planning-data/generation-information.

Australian Energy Regulator (2020, November). *Updating the Ringfencing Guidelines for Stand-Alone Power Systems and Energy Storage Devices – Issues Paper*. Retrieved from https://www.aer.gov.au/system/files/AER%20-%20Ring-fencing%20Issues%20Paper%20-%20November%202020_0.pdf.

Australian Renewable Energy Agency (2017, July). *Advancing Renewables Program*. Retrieved from https://arena.gov.au/projects/?project-value-start=0&project-value-end=200000000&technology=battery-storage.

Australian Renewable Energy Agency (2019a, May). *Gannawarra Energy Storage System (GESS)*. Retrieved from https://arena.gov.au/projects/gannawarra-energy-storage-system/.

Australian Renewable Energy Agency (2019b, August). *Victoria's first of two large-scale, grid-connected batteries reaches completion in Ballarat*. Retrieved from https://arena.gov.au/news/victorias-first-of-two-large-scale-grid-connected-batteries-reaches-completion-in-ballarat/.

ARENA Australian Renewable Energy Agency (2019c, November). *World's biggest battery grows and gains new powers*. Retrieved from https://arena.gov.au/blog/worlds-biggest-battery-grows-and-gains-new-powers/.

Australian Renewable Energy Agency (2019d, December). *Hornsdale Power Reserve Upgrade*. Retrieved from https://arena.gov.au/projects/hornsdale-power-reserve-upgrade/.

Bathurst and Strbac (2003). 'Value of combining energy storage and wind in short-term energy and balancing markets'. *Electric Power Systems Research* Vol. 67. Retrieved from: https://www.researchgate.net/publication/223017230_Value_of_combining_energy_storage_and_wind_in_short-term_energy_and_balancing_markets.

Bohn, R., Caramanis, M., & Schweppe, F. (1984). 'Optimal Pricing in Electrical Networks over Space and Time'. *The RAND Journal of Economics*, 15(3), 360–376. Retrieved January 27, 2021, from http://www.jstor.org/stable/2555444.

The Brattle Group (2018). *Market Power Screens and Mitigation Options for AESO Energy and Ancillary Services Market*. Technical Report. Retrieved from http://files.brattle.com/files/13751_market_power_screens_and_mitigation_options_for_aeso_energy_and_ancillary_service_markets.pdf.

Bushnell, J. and Novan, K. (2018). 'Setting with the sun: The impacts of renewable energy on wholesale power markets'. National Bureau of Economic Research Working Paper 24980.

California Public Utilities Commission (2020, February). *Modelling assumptions for the 2020–21 Transmission Planning Process*. Retrieved from https://www.cpuc.ca.gov/General.aspx?id=6442464144

California ISO (2019, October). *Energy Storage: Perspectives from California and Europe*. Retrieved from https://www.caiso.com/Documents/EnergyStorage-PerspectivesFromCalifornia-Europe.pdf.

California ISO (2020, February). *2019 Annual Report on Market Issues and Performance*. Retrieved from: http://www.caiso.com/market/Pages/MarketMonitoring/AnnualQuarterlyReports/Default.aspx.

Clean Energy Council (2018). *Energy Storage*. Retrieved from https://www.cleanenergycouncil.org.au/resources/technologies/energy-storage.

Climate Central (2019, November). *Is battery storage the next big thing in reducing carbon emissions?* Retrieved from https://medialibrary.climatecentral.org/resources/is-battery-storage-the-next-big-thing-in-reducing-carbon-emissions.

Cramton, P. (2017). 'Electricity market design'. *Oxford Rev. Econ. Policy* 33(4), 589–612.

Department for Energy and Mining, Government of South Australia (2019, November). 'Grid Scale Storage Fund'. Retrieved from https://www.energymining.sa.gov.au/clean_energy_transition/grid_scale_storage_fund#:~:text=The%20%2450%20million%20Grid%20Scale,of%20South%20Australia%27s%20electricity%20supplies.&text=The%20Fund%20is%20technology%20neutral.

Department of Environment, Land, Water and Planning, Government of Victoria (2020a). *Batteries and Energy Storage*. Retrieved from https://www.energy.vic.gov.au/batteries-and-energy-storage.

Department of Environment, Land, Water and Planning, Government of Victoria (2020b). *The Victorian Big Battery: Fact Sheet*. Retrieved from https://www.energy.vic.gov.au/__data/assets/pdf_file/0030/494850/The-Victorian-Big-Battery-Fact-sheet.pdf.

Department of Treasury and Finance, Government of South Australia (2017). *State Budget 2017–18: Budget Measures Statement*. Retrieved from https://www.treasury.sa.gov.au/__data/assets/pdf_file/0004/38641/2017-18_budget_measures_statement.pdf.

Edify Energy (2019). *Gannawarra Energy Storage System – Project Summary Report*. Retrieved from https://arena.gov.au/assets/2019/10/gannawarra-energy-storage-system-knowledge-sharing-report.pdf.

ElectraNet (2018, May). *ESCRI-SA Project Summary Report – The Journey to Financial Close*. Retrieved from https://www.escri-sa.com.au/globalassets/reports/escri---sa---project-summary-report---the-journey-to-financial-close---may-2018.pdf.

ElectraNet (2019, July). *ESCRI-SA Battery Energy Storage Project Operational Report #1*. Retrieved from https://arena.gov.au/assets/2016/02/escri-sa-battery-energy-storage.pdf.

ElectraNet. *Electranet's battery storage project*. Retrieved from https://www.electranet.com.au/electranets-battery-storage-project/.

EnergyAustralia (2019, June). *Ballarat Energy Storage*. Retrieved from https://www.energyaustralia.com.au/about-us/energy-generation/ballarat-battery-storage.

Energy Storage News (2017, August). *Energy storage project proposals sought for South Australia's AUS$150m renewables fund*. Retrieved from https://www.energy-storage.news/energy-storage-project-proposals-sought-for-south-australias-aus150m-renewables-fund/.

Falvi, Suzanne (2020). *Removing barriers to batteries: Key developments in market regulatory reform. Energy Source and Distribution*. Retrieved from https://esdnews.com.au/removing-barriers-to-batteries-key-developments-in-market-regulatory-reform/.

Figueiredo, Flynn and Cabral (2006). 'The Economics of Energy Storage in 14 Deregulated Power Markets'. *Energy Studies Review*, Vol. 14.

Fluence (2019, June). *Reworking the grid's circulatory system: Energy storage as a transmission asset*. Retrieved from https://blog.fluenceenergy.com/australia-energy-storage-solutions-transmission-asset.

Go, Roderick S., Francisco D. Munoz, and Jean-Paul Watson (2016). 'Assessing the economic value of co-optimized grid-scale energy storage investments in supporting high renewable portfolio standards.' *Applied Energy* 183: 902–913.

Graf, C., Quaglia, F., and Wolak, F.A. (2020). 'Simplified electricity market models with significant intermittent renewable capacity: Evidence from Italy'. National Bureau of Economic Research Working Paper 27262.

Graves, F., Jenkins, T. and Murphy, D. (1999). 'Opportunities for Electricity Storage in Deregulating Markets'. *The Electricity Journal*, Vol. 12, pp. 46–56. Retrieved from: https://www.sciencedirect.com/science/article/abs/pii/S1040619099000718.

Harvey, S.M. and Hogan, W.W. (2000). 'Nodal and Zonal Congestion Management and the Exercise of Market Power'. Unpublished Manuscript, Center for Business and Government, Kennedy School of Government, Harvard University. Retrieved from http://lmpmarketdesign.com/papers/zonal_jan10.pdf.

Hessami, M. and Bowly, D. (2011). 'Economic Feasibility and optimisation of an energy storage system for Portland Wind Farm (Victoria, Australia)'. *Applied Energy* 88(8): 2755–2763.

Hogan, W.W. (1999). 'Transmission Congestion: The Nodal-Zonal Debate Revisited'. Unpublished Manuscript, Center for Business and Government, Kennedy School of Government, Harvard University. Retrieved from https://scholar.harvard.edu/whogan/files/nezn0227.pdf.

Infigen Energy (2020, September). *Lake Bonney BESS – Project Summary Report*. Retrieved from https://arena.gov.au/assets/2020/10/infigen-lake-bonney-project-summary-report.pdf.

Jenkin, T. and Weiss, J. (2005). 'Estimating the Value of Electricity Storage: Some Size, Location and Market Structure Issues'. *Electricity Storage Applications and Technologies Conference*, San Francisco.

Jha, A. and Leslie, G. (2019). 'Dynamic Costs and Market Power: The Rooftop Solar Transition in Western Australia'. Unpublished Manuscript. Retrieved from https://economics-events.sydney.edu.au/wp-content/uploads/2019/10/Jha_Leslie_WA.pdf.

Katzen, Matthew and Leslie, Gordon (2020). 'Siting and Operating Incentives in Electrical Networks: A Study of Mispricing in Australia's Zonal Market'. Retrieved from https://ssrn.com/abstract=3501336.

Kirkpatrick, A. Justin (2020). *Estimating Congestion Benefits of Batteries for Unobserved Networks: A Machine Learning Approach.* Michigan State University.

Leslie, G.W., Stern, D.I., Shanker, A., and Hogan, M.T. (2020). 'Designing electricity markets for high penetrations of zero or low marginal cost intermittent energy sources', *The Electricity Journal*, Vol. 33, Issue 9, 106847.

Mallapragada, D.S., Sepulveda, N.A., and Jenkins, J.D. (2020). 'Long-run system value of battery energy storage in future grids with increasing wind and solar generation'. *Applied Energy, 275*, 115390.

National Renewable Energy Laboratory (2020, August). *Annual Technology Baseline: Electricity.* Neoen.

Neoen (2020). *South Australia's Big Battery.* Retrieved from https://hornsdalepowerreserve.com.au/.

Premier of Victoria (2020, May). '*Moorabool to Host Australia's Biggest Battery*'. Retrieved from https://www.premier.vic.gov.au/moorabool-host-australias-biggest-battery.

Potomac Economics (2019). *2018 State of the Market Report for the ERCOT Electricity Markets.* Retrieved from https://www.potomaceconomics.com/wp-content/uploads/2019/06/2018-State-of-the-Market-Report.pdf.

Powerlink (2019, September). *Expanding NSW–QLD Transmission Transfer Capacity.* Retrieved from https://www.powerlink.com.au/sites/default/files/2019-09/Expanding%20NSW-QLD%20Transmission%20Transfer%20Capacity%20PADR%20%E2%80%93%20PADR%20Full%20Report.pdf.

PV Magazine Australia (2020, November). '*Vic Big Battery to Unlock Renewables*'. Retrieved from https://www.pv-magazine-australia.com/2020/11/05/vic-big-battery-to-unlock-renewables-in-the-state/.

Smart Energy Council (2018, September). *Australian energy storage: Market analysis.* Retrieved from https://www.smartenergy.org.au/sites/default/files/uploaded-content/field_f_content_file/australian_energy_storage_market_analysis_report_sep18_final.pdf.

Solar Choice (2014, January). *Are falling battery costs the solution to solar PV ills?* Retrieved from https://www.solarchoice.net.au/blog/news/are-falling-battery-costs-the-solution-to-solar-pv-ills-310114/.

Staffell, I. and Rustomji, M. (2016). '*Maximising the value of electricity storage*'. *Journal of Energy Storage*, Retrieved from: https://www.researchgate.net/publication/307614118_Maximising_the_value_of_electricity_storage.

TransGrid (2020a, December). *Wallgrove Grid Battery.* Retrieved from https://www.transgrid.com.au/wallgrovebattery.

TransGrid (2020b, December). *Wallgrove Grid Battery Project – Developing innovative solutions for the future grid.* Retrieved from https://www.transgrid.com.au/what-we-do/projects/current-projects/Wallgrove/Documents/TRAN_301025_Wallgrove%20Grid%20Battery%20Project%20Fact%20Sheet_FA%20WEB.pdf.

University of Queensland (2020, May). *The business case for behind-the-meter energy storage. Q1 performance of UQ's 1.1MW Tesla battery.* Retrieved from https://sustainability.uq.edu.au/files/11868/EPBQtyRptq12020.pdf.

US Energy Information Administration (2020, July). *Battery storage in the United States: An update on market trends.* Retrieved from https://www.eia.gov/analysis/studies/electricity/batterystorage/.

WattClarity (2020, March). *Surviving on the island – again*. Retrieved from
https://wattclarity.com.au/articles/2020/03/surviving-on-the-island-again/.

Wolak, F.A. (2019). 'The role of efficient pricing in enabling a low-carbon electricity
sector'. *Economics of Energy & Environmental Policy, 8*(2), 29–52.

Chapter 5

The Market Design Imperative

Guillaume Roger[1]

1.   Introduction

Buying and selling power

In the National Electricity Market (NEM), power is bought and sold in a centralised wholesale market that resembles a double auction. In a double auction, sellers make bids to sell and buyers make bids to buy. The bids to buy ordered in decreasing value constitute a demand function; likewise, bids to sell (in an increasing order) constitute a supply function. Ignoring some (at times important) details, the market clears when the buying offer price is no higher than the selling offer price, that is, where supply and demand cross.

The NEM is a costly simplification of a double auction. Sellers (generators) make bids to sell energy but buyers *typically* do not make bids to buy – most of the load capacity remains unscheduled, as for example retailers.[2] Instead these loads simply express a quantity demanded, not a bid made of a price and quantity pair, or the market operator relies on a forecast of the quantity demanded. The sum of quantities is the aggregate demand. This simplification of the demand side implies the aggregate demand is highly inelastic. The market clears where the supply function (also called 'bid stack') meets this quantity.

---

1   **Guillaume Roger**, Co-Director, Grid Innovation Hub; Associate Director, Monash Energy Institute; Associate Professor, Monash University, Melbourne.

2   Some large industrial loads are scheduled, and so do express a demand function, but not many. As of writing, for example, Monash University campuses, on which tens of thousands of people work every day, are not scheduled loads.

The clearing price is the one that corresponds to the last selling bid that is accepted – also called the marginal bid. This description sets aside important technical constraints on transmission, which may be subject to congestions. Subject to these transmission constraints, generators are dispatched according to the merit order – simply from the cheapest to the most expensive. A generator must be dispatched to earn revenue.

Of course, even if it is inelastic in the short run, the demand can vary enormously depending on the time of the day and the day of the year, but it is not a responsive function of price. These variations in demand are concentrated on the inelastic part of the supply curve, that is, where producing more electricity is increasingly expensive. Put together, these two facts induce wide variations in prices, as shown in the figures below by way of example.

Figure 1: NSW pool prices over 48 half-hour intervals

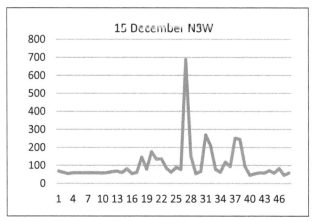

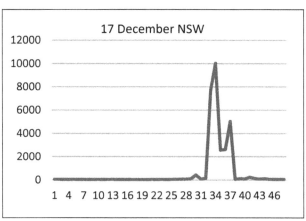

Source: AEMO. Author's figures.

On 15 December 2020 in NSW, the clearing price reached \$686/MW, and as much as \$10034/MW on 17 December; this is a far cry from the average of \$115/MW for the period – which is considered very high already by international standards. The simplification of the double auction is costly because the aggregate demand is invariant in price; in the short run it is inelastic. Hence the only degree of freedom to clear the market is for the price to increase. This makes for sustainably high prices, as well as volatile prices.

Market design

Market design is concerned with finding the (economically) most efficient allocation of resources between parties willing to trade; this allocation may be, for example, the welfare-maximising allocation. To achieve this, it relies on an allocation rule, a transfer rule (a price or multiple prices) and an exclusion rule. This problem is invariant to technology. For example, an English auction allocates the object to the highest bidder (allocation rule). This bidder pays the bid they offered; other bidders receive nothing and pay nothing (transfer rule), and bidders must register before bidding (exclusion rule). This auction format may be used to purchase houses, works of art or second-hand golf clubs on the internet. Depending on the particulars of the problem, it may be the optimal auction format, but it need not be. Whether it is the optimal auction format depends on what the auctioneer wants to achieve (e.g. revenue maximisation, welfare maximisation or any other criterion), the particulars of the object(s) to sell, whether multiple units may be sold, whether the auction is repeated, whether there are multiple sellers, the risk attitude of bidders and so on. Thus, market design is a problem that is best treated on a case-by-case basis. There is no general theorem we can readily rely on, bar the principle that the details matter.

Costs have very little to do with market design; they only determine a lower bound on price (the transfer rule) in that sellers typically prefer not selling at a loss. The reason for this (almost) irrelevance of costs is that a well-crafted market design seeks to solicit *valuations* from bidders.[3] Even if the cost of energy production is zero, the valuation by consumers is certainly not (always) zero. Hence designing markets for zero-marginal cost generators is not difficult *per se*. The difficulty is rather the fact that different generation technologies are characterised by *different* costs, which condition their bidding behaviour. This includes dynamic costs, that is, costs that evolve over time;

---

3   In the NEM equilibrium prices may fall below marginal cost at times, however, for other reasons such as fixed costs, or ramp-up costs.

an example of dynamic costs is ramp-up costs. Dealing with dynamic costs requires enriching the bidding space, which is currently limited to 5-minute increments; this is nothing that cannot be done by modifying the exact market rules. That is, after all, the point of market design.

Modern electricity generation (and storage) technologies possess characteristics that render the current market design in use in the NEM obsolete. That design is suited to a stable production technology that operates in a competitive environment, not to a world of intermittent generation that lacks inertia. These new and emerging technologies also present new challenges to market designers, such as what to do with electricity storage. Thankfully, there is a considerable literature on market design, some of which has informed the design of markets that are currently operating, including electricity markets. In October 2020, Robert Wilson and Paul Milgrom were famously awarded the Nobel Prize in economics for their work on market design. The works of Wilson and Milgrom, and many of their colleagues, can be used to inform us as we confront these new challenges.

2. The wholesale market today

The NEM is an energy-only spot market, which means that selling capacity or reserves does not occur in the open market, and that bids are relevant for immediate delivery only.[4, 5] It is supported by a market for ancillary services that assist with frequency control; this market remains small in comparison. Generators and loads can enter into futures contracts, which are mostly contracts for differences in prices. Other jurisdictions include capacity markets (e.g. Western Australia), in which generators are paid for being ready to operate, and day-ahead markets (e.g. New York), in which generators can make binding bids for future delivery.

The process of bidding in the spot market to supply electricity is repeated every five minutes, and relies on the merit order for clearing and dispatch. However, even though the 'auction' is repeated every five minutes, it is designed as a one-off auction. Yet we know, simply from using eBay for example, that repeated auctions are not the same as a one-off auction. The current auction design also

---

4   The market operator (AEMO) may procure reserves via bilateral agreements, not in the open market.

5   More precisely, the NEM features a pre-dispatch schedule, which is formed on the basis of bids collected by the market operator 24 hours in advance. However, this schedule is informative and not binding, and bids can be withdrawn or amended for spot delivery; and they are.

ignores the fact that most generators cannot decide to sell instantaneously; they experience start-up costs and ramp-up costs.[6] Finally, the current design rests on the assumption of competitive bidding by generators. While there is a large number of plants supplying the NEM, they vary considerably in size. Large plants can exercise unilateral market power; they can move prices, and so can extract rents. In addition, the ownership of these many plants is highly concentrated, with firms like AGL, EnergyAustralia and Origin Energy controlling approximately three-quarters of the total generation capacity. This concentration not only aggregates unilateral market power; it also invites coordinated bidding within firms, as well as across firms. This reality is not accounted for in the current bidding process, nor in the market oversight.

These deficiencies are not just theoretical or stylistic; they have real implications for prices. Using ABS data, the two charts below display a time series of wholesale prices for the states of NSW and Victoria. Over a twenty-year period, these prices have increased almost four-fold in these two states. In that time capacity has fluctuated, sometimes famously: generators have left and entered the market. Likewise, fuel prices have oscillated: coal and gas prices have increased and decreased. And of course, renewable generation has developed. Yet the persistent feature in the wholesale market over these last two decades is the sustained rise in the price of electricity well in excess of inflation.

There may be multiple, and not mutually exclusive, explanations for this perennial price increase. Political interference has been blamed; likewise, the lack of government intervention has been blamed. There is no denying that the lack of coherent government policy is not helping. However, more culprits may lie elsewhere too.

The concentration in generation and the rise of 'gen-tailers' (vertical integration) is a significant source of concern. Gans and Wolak (2007) show in fact that coordination in bidding is not even necessary for wholesale prices to increase. It is sufficient to have an uncontracted hedge in the retail market, which many generators acquired by vertical integration (with retailers). Concentration (the fact that few firms own many generators) compounds this problem in that it augments the incentives for the unilateral use of market power, and also opens the door to coordinated bidding.

---

6   Start-up and ramp-up characteristics may be accounted for as constraints in the optimal dispatch. This is different than expressing their cost as part of the bidding process. These start-up and ramp-up costs are implicitly accounted for in the bidding decisions of generators, of course. However, dispatch remains uncertain; therefore these bid prices also include an insurance premium. They are higher than necessary.

Figure 2: Yearly average pool prices for Victoria and New South Wales, 1998 to 2019

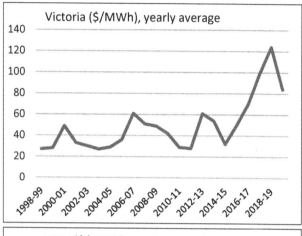

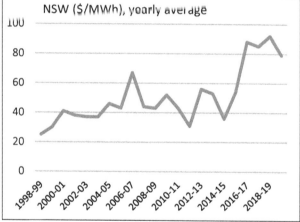

Source: AEMO. Author's figures.

While vertical integration and horizontal concentration are problems of industrial organisation and competition policy, their reality is not accounted for in the wholesale bidding design, nor in any ancillary rules. In addition, the vertical integration of generators and retailers renders (at least a fraction of) the contract market redundant. Because AGL, for example, is the party on both sides of the one trade, it need not care at which (wholesale) price power is transacted.[7] A less active contract market easily becomes a barrier to entry for both generators and retailers that do not benefit from this vertical

---

7   Even if its generators must bid into the NEM and its retail arm purchase from the NEM, this is still just a matter of 'transfer pricing'.

integration. More recently, the lack of 'demand-response' has (finally) been attracting some attention. Because so little of the capacity is consumed by scheduled loads, demand in the wholesale market remains largely inelastic. This lack of elasticity makes for higher prices than really necessary, regardless of market structure; a market that severely lacks competition makes matters only worse.

Finally, in a new paper, Jha and Leslie (2020) show that the combination of solar power generation and the dynamic costs of alternative generators (gas turbines) induces both higher volatility in price and higher average prices in Western Australia. This is the now famous 'duck curve', which is fast turning into a 'swan curve'. The problem can be traced back to market design.[8] The 5-minute pricing rule provides no incentives for gas turbines to turn on early and fails to deal with the well-known unit commitment problem, but then lets them exercise their market power unfettered.[9]

Perhaps the most significant challenge for wholesale bidding in the NEM is the transition to renewable generation. Renewable energy is intermittent, difficult to forecast, difficult to control, and some of its sources covary strongly, thus making for feast or famine. At present, a necessary complement to renewable generation is a peaking technology such as an open-cycle gas turbine to provide electricity when the renewable source cannot operate. However, even if these technologies are well understood, Jha and Leslie (2020) show their integration is far from obvious when the bidding rules are not designed to accommodate them.

Looking into the future, a more natural complement to renewable energy is storage, which allows for intertemporal substitution of production to match the consumption profile. Storage creates the opportunity for arbitrage in the physical market, and so holds great prospects for price smoothing as well. Storage is also very helpful in ancillary markets, such as frequency controls. Finally, storage can 'firm' renewable energy sources, which are considered non-dispatchable at present, and thus turn them into dispatchable capacity. However, integrating storage into the NEM requires a significant redesign of

---

8   In addition to the obviously distortionary feed-in tariffs and net-metering arrangements mandated by state regulators.

9   The unit commitment problem is the difficult decision generators face whether to start up and ramp up knowing they may not be dispatched, and so may fail to generate revenue. In a different context, Lindsay and Goeree (2020) refer to this as the 'exposure problem'; they show a combinatorial auction improves greatly on a simple auction because the combinatorial auction is effectively a contingent contract.

the entire wholesale market for three main reasons. First, at any point in time storage can buy or sell energy. Therefore, with storage a bid must be clearly identified as a bid to buy or a bid to sell. This requires the demand side of the market to become active, that is, for a demand schedule to be expressed.[10] Second, while the patterns of peak renewable energy production (afternoon) and peak demand are well understood and can be reliably forecast, there is no market mechanism that allows storage operators to exploit the systematic price differences these patterns generate. Third, charging and discharging decisions depend on the state of charge of a battery and on the expectations of the storage unit operator as to future prices. Given that other storage operators face the same problem, the bidding process becomes what economists call a *stochastic dynamic game*. As long as there are only a few storage units, the dynamic nature of this game can be ignored at some small cost only. But this is unlikely to be true when storage becomes a large fraction of the dispatchable capacity. How to clear such a market is an open question.

The corollary of this discussion is the need to also redesign the dispatch engine. The current dispatch (NEMDE) is based on a linear program that delivers an optimal static dispatch based on the spot supply function (subject to constraints). This dispatch engine is unable to solve a dynamic optimisation problem. Hence new methods are called for to implement the optimal dispatch.

3.   Redesigning the market

Section 2 suggests it is not surprising to observe poor market outcomes. The rules of the market are inadequate to the times and to the technologies that are emerging very rapidly. Market rules and market structure are man-made; they can be altered to be better suited to the current reality of the electricity market. Overhauling the wholesale market should address multiple objectives. A new design should:

- Foster activity in the forward market;
- Internalise market power, concentration and coordinated bidding;
- Restore demand elasticity;
- Address the dynamic costs of supply;
- Properly integrate storage.

---

10   Currently a storage unit is registered as a load and a generator simultaneously, which addresses the need to express a demand schedule. However, it is not clear what happens upon dispatch if the storage unit bids to buy or sell in the same time interval.

Fortunately, these multiple objectives are not mutually exclusive; further-more, they can be achieved using conceptually, if not technically, simple solutions.

A.   The forward market, unilateral market power and prices

The progressive vertical integration of retailers into 'gen-tailers' made a sig-nificant fraction of the forward market redundant, with two effects. First, the lack of supply and liquidity in the forward market may be a barrier to entry for both independent generators and independent retailers. For example, Roger (2018) documents that the turnover of electricity futures on the ASX decreases from 400% of physical delivery in 2011 down to 200% in 2015–16. Even at 400% of physical delivery this does not make for a very active market; oil futures are traded much more actively with a turnover of around 1230% of deliveries worldwide in 2011. Such a low turnover, in spite of very high price volatility, suggests it is difficult to find a counterparty. Without a counter-party, independent generators and retailers may find it too risky to enter this (very volatile) energy market. Second, vertical integration also pushed up wholesale clearing prices, as had been predicted by Gans and Wolak (2007). This empirical fact is consistent with what theory tells us of forward markets; typically, they are pro-competitive, as first shown by Allaz and Vila (1993) and many since, including by the work of Wolak (2000). Newberry (1995) argues that the contract market is an avenue to maintain competition in the long term – precisely because it facilitates entry. So do Crampton and Ausubel (2009), adding that an active forward market coordinates investment in the medium term and ensures reliability in the long run. The idea is that, just as with interest rate futures, electricity futures prices are a reliable signal of future energy prices. Investors can then use them to formulate reliable estimates of their future revenue.

Absent (active) forward markets, any generator is prone to engage in uni-lateral price manipulation, as observed by Biggar (2011). This echoes Wolak's (2004) earlier observation, who writes that 'It is difficult to conceive of an industry more susceptible to the exercise of unilateral market power than electricity'. Indeed, the conditions are ideal:

- Most loads (retailers) are not scheduled, and so are price inelastic.
- Intertemporal substitution (storage) is still almost impossible.
- Generation capacity is fixed in the short run.
- There are large returns to scale.
- Transmission constraints may bind, thus creating local monopolies.

Furthermore, antitrust law in Australia does not specifically prohibit the exercise of market power. None of this means that firms holding unilateral market power should be left to their own devices; the use of market power can remain socially harmful, especially when it comes to electricity.

In Singapore, the Energy Market Company (the local operator) solved the twin problem of excessive market power in generation and of vertical integration by mandating *vesting contracts*; the vesting regime extends to entities that are vertically integrated as well. These vesting contracts are mandatory for generators wanting to participate in the wholesale market, which are required to offer a specified fraction of their capacity to retailers at a negotiated price for future delivery. They clearly resemble forward contracts, most of which are bilateral contracts anyway in Australia. They certainly possess the same incentive properties as forward contracts, which are known to promote competition.[11] Thus reserving a fraction of capacity to vesting contracts can be used as a substitute to an active contract market and promote competition.

B.   Local market power, concentration and coordinated bidding

Vesting contracts may tame the *unilateral* exercise of market power in the wholesale market but they are likely unable to prevent the exercise of (unilateral) market power arising *locally* out of transmission constraints and insufficient to deter *coordinated* bidding by individual plants owned by the same entity.

Local market power emerges routinely on electricity grids because parts of the network become congested. In this case, only the generator(s) that are unaffected by the congestion can be dispatched, regardless of the merit-order. In such a case they are, for a time, a monopoly. Such a problem arises regardless of the settlement regime: it may occur in a zonal market as well as in a nodal market. Wolak (2004) suggests to equip the regulator, or the market operator, with a local market power mitigation mechanism, whereby a threshold for intervention and a settlement regime are defined. The progressive introduction of nodal pricing around the world has made it plain that such a mechanism is necessary.

At present, both the market design and the dispatch engine presume competitive bidding consistent with supplying energy at (or close to) short-run marginal cost. However, this is clearly not in line with the reality of the

---

11   With forward sales the residual supply to offer is reduced. Therefore, the inframarginal loss arising from lowering prices (to be more competitive) is smaller. The trade-off between inframarginal loss and marginal gain takes place at a larger aggregate quantity and at a lower price.

industrial organisation of the market. Approximately three-quarters of the capacity supplied in the NEM is owned by three entities – AGL, Origin and EnergyAustralia. This leaves little doubt as to the nature of competition in the NEM.

Newberry (1995) observes that a handful of generators can exercise market power to the benefit of many. In its simplest form, this coordination enables the owning entity to internalise the inframarginal losses of all its plants; this is the same effect as bidding with a single large plant. To see this, suppose the clearing price is p and consider a seller withholding capacity on one of its n generators – plant j – by shutting it down. Then the clearing price becomes $p_w \geq p$. Without withholding, the total payoff to the seller is $\Sigma_i(p-c_i)q_i$ and with withholding it is $\Sigma_{i \neq j}(p_w-c_i)q_i$, so the gains and losses are:

$$\Sigma_{i \neq j}(p_w-p)q_i \text{ versus } (p-c_j)q_j.$$

In words, by forgoing the net profit on plant j, the owner can collect an additional margin p_w-p over the quantities sold by the other $n-1$ plants. The effect is the same as with unilateral market power – increasing the price by withholding quantities – however, with a large portfolio of plants, this trade-off is much more likely to be profitable. As noted by Wolak (2004), the exercise of (unilateral) market power is very difficult to detect: wholesale prices do vary widely for good reasons; making the difference between exercising 'too much' market power and just responding to incentives is an almost impossible task. It is likely even more difficult when multiple plants are owned by the same entity; for example, is plant j idle to manipulate the market, or because it is really in need of maintenance?

In addition, with a diversified portfolio, the owning entity can select *which* plant to suppress: typically, the higher cost one, which induces the smaller marginal loss (the term $(p-c_j)q_j$) and is nearest the marginal (clearing) bid. Finally, in a double auction it is enough for the marginal plant to restrain its bidding; all the inframarginal bidders benefit from the higher prices this practice induces. Admittedly this last step does require a measure of coordination that is not always easy to reach, but it is eminently feasible. For example, Byrne and de Roos (2019) document the high degree of co-ordination gasoline retailers achieve in their price-setting in Australia. It is easy to see that generators have even stronger incentives to coordinate than gasoline retailers: they face a unique clearing price.

Newberry's (1995) prescription to solve this issue is for owners of multiple plants to be forced to divest. This natural remedy belongs to the rule book of competition policy, rather than market design. It has been extensively used, in act and in threat, in the United States. However, Australia has been reluctant to impose compulsory divestiture; it is a policy that is unlikely to be pursued at the time of writing. Short of this course of action, it is left to the design of the market and to market oversight to internalise the fact that bidders not only hold unilateral market power, but also can coordinate their bidding strategies. Most obviously this calls for heightened oversight of market operations by a body such as the Australian Energy Regulator, or the market operator (AEMO). Wolak (2004) again suggests to ask the regulator to rapidly curb behaviour that is detrimental to system reliability and market efficiency. This proposal relies essentially on *retrospective* measures that require measuring departures from historical 'competitive' benchmarks, and taking corrective action. In the context of coordinated bidding, this may ask the counterfactual question 'What bids should we have seen from Firm X that we did not see, and what is the damage from this departure from expected behaviour?' Of course, defining the counterfactual bidding profile, which is the basis for determining whether a transgression occurred and also to compute damages, entails a measure of uncertainty and may be open to dispute. It is also technically demanding but a government and its agencies that are committed to market transparency should be eager to make the investment in human resources to perform this kind of analysis. Compared to what is at stake, hiring this talent remains cheap.

A last avenue may be to borrow from APRA (Australian Prudential Regulation Agency), which essentially took to regulating the format of executive compensation in the institutions it supervises. APRA requires the boards of the entities they supervise to document how they derive their executive compensation, what criteria this compensation may be conditioned on, that it includes claw-back conditions, and so on. The idea is that executive compensation is in place to induce certain behaviour, and APRA wants to make sure this behaviour is not deleterious to the system as a whole. Likewise, a body like the AER may ask of entities owning more than one generation plant that the compensation of each plant manager be solely tied to the performance of that plant, and not with the overall performance of the owning entity. This would unwind at least some of the benefits from coordinated bidding.

C. Demand elasticity

Electricity is almost surely the only commodity that has a demand which is largely inelastic; that is, how much electricity a user demands is broadly invariant in its price. This is clearly not the case for cars or electronics, for example. This lack of price responsiveness is an artefact of market design, as well as an accident of history.

At the retail level, electricity consumption is measured periodically at the meter, and between two measurement periods no information can be sent to consumers. Until smart meters are introduced, there is no way to measure the *timing* of consumption; therefore, real-time pricing, even if desirable, is not yet feasible – with the notable exception of the state of Victoria. The inability to measure the timing of consumption also leaves retailers without any demand information with which to formulate their own demand in the wholesale market. Instead they, or the market operator, must formulate a forecast of it. At the wholesale level the market design is also stifled in some sense. Except for a small number of industrial loads ('scheduled' loads), only a quantity demanded (say, Q) is forecast rather than a full demand schedule (say $Q(p)$) being actually expressed. Because the aggregate demand is essentially inelastic in the short run, only the supply can adjust. This implies higher price volatility, as well as no meaningful quantity adjustment in the face of higher prices. This stands in contrast to almost any other market, where the equilibrium quantity decreases when price increases. This is shown in the figures below. On the left-hand side demand is inelastic and quantities do not change as the supply shifts leftward (supplying becomes more expensive); on the right-hand side, the equilibrium quantity decreases as the cost of supply increases. This mitigates market power and tames the price increase in equilibrium. In addition, it is clear that more capacity is always required on the left-hand side than the right-hand side; that capacity is costly.

Figure 3: The quantity impact of demand elasticity

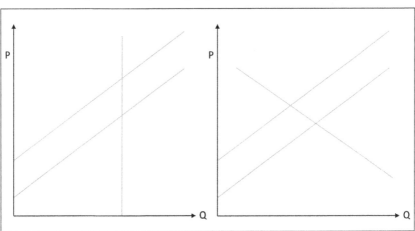

Source: Author

At the time of writing, a great deal of effort and money have been poured into trying to restore some demand elasticity under the moniker of 'demand response'. For example, ARENA funded a pilot study run by AGL to implement 'demand response' by offering households financial incentives to reduce their consumption in times of high demand, or to turn over control of their devices to the AGL. It is easy to see that this is completely equivalent to having a price-elastic demand, but it is much more costly.

At least two elements are required to restore demand elasticity. The first one is the measurement of the timing of consumption at the retail level, ideally together with real-time pricing. This is easily achieved with the smart meters currently in use in Victoria, and their deployment can be extended to other states. Even without real-time pricing, retailers can formulate a better forecast of demand with the information these meters can supply. Real-time pricing is known to induce a more efficient allocation and the socially correct investment level – see Borenstein (2005) and references therein. Of course, real-time pricing also conveys to retailers the true aggregate demand of their consumers, which is the information they need for their own bidding.[12] Furthermore, in a recent paper, Leslie, Pourkhanali and Roger (2020) show that real-time pricing is fairer and more equitable, especially to more vulnerable households (elderly, tenants, migrants and lower income), which may sound counter to common wisdom. The reason is the *timing* of consumption: these households consume comparatively more when electricity is cheap to produce, and comparatively less when it is expensive. Thus, efficiency and distributional concerns agree when it comes to electricity use, and both can be achieved by using real-time pricing. This should make it an easy reform to achieve.

The second element required to restore demand elasticity is the introduction of a true double auction, in which retailers, as well as other large loads, can express their demand schedule. That is, for any time interval, the quantity demanded may vary with price, as expressed by consumers. This requires that retailers be able to bid price–quantity pairs, as finely as possible.[13] The aggregation of these price–quantity pairs is the (now elastic) demand function, just like the aggregation of price–quantity pairs bid by generators is the supply function.

---

12 Real-time pricing need not expose consumers to the full price volatility to induce some elasticity; *some* response may be sufficient. In addition, retailers can also offer insurance to risk-averse consumers. These insurance contracts can be constructed to limit expenses, yet still leave a modicum of demand responsiveness.

13 Sometimes this is referred to as a 'two-sided' market, which is a misnomer. It is really a double auction.

D.   Day-ahead and dynamic costs

Day-ahead markets feature prominently in large overseas markets such as New York, the Pennsylvania–New Jersey–Maryland market or California. In brief, generators make *binding* supply offers for a 24-hour window in advance (the day ahead), and a spot ('balancing') market is used to balance actual demand and supply in real time. This construction presents three benefits. First, while the balancing market may be volatile, it remains small and so this volatility only affects the marginal quantities of the balancing market. Thus price movements of the balancing markets only have a small impact on the total cost of supplying electricity. Second, a day-ahead structure is in effect a forward market and so it displays the same features as a forward market. In particular, it possesses the same incentive properties as a forward (contract) market. Because the inframarginal units are presold (at the ahead price), the inframarginal effect is weaker: the firms are less concerned about the (negative) impact of a price reduction on their (inframarginal) units. As a result, competition for the marginal units in the balancing market is fiercer, just like competition in the spot market is fiercer when some quantities are already sold in the forward market. In turn this enhances competition in the ahead market.

Third, and perhaps the most important feature, a day-ahead market allows optimisation of the dispatch over a 24-hour horizon, rather than a 5-minute window, and so is better able to accommodate dynamic costs (ramping costs). Dynamic costs were long not an issue, not because they did not exist but because they could be ignored. Indeed, all thermal technologies feature dynamic costs; however, as long as they remain uninterrupted, these dynamic costs can be amortised over a long duration and so matter little to price movements. Dynamic costs become an issue when they must be repeatedly incurred. Recently, renewable energy sources have been able to increasingly displace thermal generation during the day thanks to the combination of low marginal cost and a myopic market design that prices and dispatches energy in 5-minute increments. However, in any given day, eventually, thermal generators have to be activated and ramping cost have to be incurred. The result is that prices become increasingly volatile over time. Moreover, only the most expensive technologies (OCGT) can afford to keep up with this pattern. This phenomenon has been well documented by Jha and Leslie (2020) in Western Australia. Because thermal generators have to stop and restart more frequently, not only does volatility increase, so does the average price of electricity. Thus, paradoxically, the introduction of low-cost technologies contributes to increasing prices in the NEM – because of an inadequate market design.

Regardless of a technical solution (such as storage, for example), this situation can be greatly improved by re-designing the market to account for the reality of dynamic costs. These dynamic costs induce some form of inter-temporal complementarities in the production of electricity. Complementarities render the bidding for *bundles* comparatively more attractive to the bidder; here bundles are multiple generation intervals. Below is a fictitious example for illustration: consider a thermal technology with a positive marginal cost (MC), and a renewable technology with zero marginal cost. The first table supposes a 5-minute settlement only, with corresponding bidding over three such periods.

Table 1: Illustration of standard bid and dispatch

	Period 1	Period 2	Period 3	Revenue
Total demand	100MW	150MW	250MW	
Clearing price	$20	≥$30	≥$30	
Thermal capacity 250MW	MC=$10	MC=$10	MC=$10	≥$9000
	Ramp=$10	Ramp=$20	Ramp=$20	
	Revenue=0	Revenue≥$1500	Revenue≥$7500	
Renewable 100MW	Revenue=$2000	Revenue≥$3000	0 – no production	≥$5000
Total revenue				≥$14,000

In this first example, the thermal generator is completely displaced because of the merit-order effect in the first period; only the renewable operator supplies. Consequently, the thermal generator must ramp up faster in the second period, during which it supplies the residual 50MW of power; thanks to the merit-order effect, the renewable generator supplies its whole capacity of 100MW. In the last period, only the thermal technology operates. The total payment to generators is at least $14000. Revenues are computed supposing a clearing price of $30 in periods 2 and 3, and so are in fact a lower bound.

Ahead markets can enrich the bidding space because they allow the designer to create *bundles* of generation intervals, and so can be part of the solution to this problem.[14] For example, a bundle may be a production commitment for two or three periods, or to produce different quantities for two or three periods. One notes that, under this design, bidding for a single generation

---

14   This is borrowing from combinatorial auctions.

interval, or a collection of generation intervals, is always possible. That is, an ahead market with bundles of complementary units does not remove any bidding options; it only adds options that can be useful to some generators. The second table below illustrates the point. Here the thermal generator commits to supplying at $25/MW for the first *two* periods. For simplicity, the same price of $25/MW is used as the unique clearing price. The essential point is that because the ramp-up rate is slower in period 2, it is cheaper. The ramp-up rate is slower in period 2 because the generator already supplies in period 1.

Table 2: Illustration of combinatorial bid and dispatch

	Period 1	Period 2	Period 3	Revenue
Total demand	100MW	150MW	250MW	
Clearing price	$25	$25	≥$30	
Thermal capacity 250MW	MC=$10	MC=$10	MC=$10	≥$10,625
	Ramp=$10	Ramp=$10	Ramp=$20	
	Revenue=$1250	Revenue=$1875	Revenue≥$7500	
Renewable 100MW	Revenue=$1250	Revenue=$1875	0 – no production	$3125
Total revenue				≥$13,750

Now the merit order is *ignored* period to period. Instead the dispatcher considers the least-cost combination over the *entire* three-period horizon. Optimally, dispatch is evenly split between the two technologies in the first two periods; hence they receive the same revenue. The total transfer to generators decreases to $13,750. It is *optimal* to *not* enforce the (static) merit order to minimise total costs to consumers. If the dispatch did enforce the static merit order we would revert to the situation in the first table.

The day-ahead market is a simple and convenient implementation of a *combinatorial* market, in which generators bid to supply bundles; this is exactly the example of Tables 1 and 2. Lindsay and Goeree (2020) show that using bundles, which effectively act as contingent contracts, alleviates the 'exposure problem'. The exposure problem is one that involves a series of sequential trades, some outcome of which may leave some traders worse off; for example, selling a house and not being able to buy another one. Allowing for bundles renders every transaction contingent on other (necessary) transactions also taking place. In electricity markets this phenomenon is called the unit commitment problem; a generator may ramp up but not be dispatched. Like in the example in the table, a generator prefers ramping up if it knows it will be dispatched; this certainty even has a price in that the generator can afford to bid more aggressively then. Bichlera, Fux and Goeree (2018) implement a combinatorial exchange for fishing licenses to again solve the 'exposure problem' for the Government of New South Wales. Of course, combinatorial bidding can easily be extended to loads seeking to purchase certain bundles of energy, as it was to both sides of the market by Bichlera, Fux and Goeree (2018).

Detractors of combinatorial bidding procedures point to the computational burden they naturally generate. Indeed, for a single generator making decisions to supply over 48 half-hour windows, there are in excess of 281 trillion combinations to consider (2^{48}). However, many of these combinations are in fact irrelevant and so can be ruled out of the problem. For example, a combination such as ON-OFF-ON-OFF-ON can be excluded: first, it is extremely unlikely it would ever be selected by the generator and, second, it is likely to not be encouraged by the market operator. By focusing on 'contiguous' combinations resembling ON ON ON OFF-OFF, the number of relevant bundles can be greatly decreased. For example, halving the number of options to consider (now 2^{24}) brings the number of combinations to less than 16.8 million. This brief discussion also makes it plain that the details of a combinatorial market must be carefully worked out for it to deliver the correct incentives while remaining feasible. Finally, while a day-ahead market need not be a combinatorial market, it would be a missed opportunity to not take advantage of the day-ahead design to also include the combinatorial aspects.

The examples of Tables 1 and 2 bring forth a potential downside of the combinatorial market: what to do with the spare capacity of the renewable generator (50MW in period 1, 25MW in period 2)? One solution of course is to produce the energy and store it, to which we turn next.

E.   Integrating storage

Investment in grid-scale storage has been increasing very fast in Australia. Since Neoen invested in the Hornsdale Power Reserve, it doubled down in Victoria with the Big Battery (Neoen media release, 5 November 2020). Around the same time, AGL also indicated it would invest in large batteries located next to the Torrens power station in South Australia and on the Liddell site in NSW; this was confirmed in March 2021 (AGL media release, 14 August 2020, and the *Australian Financial Review*, 24 March 2021). These large-scale batteries are complemented by smaller facilities, which typically operate not in the merchant model, but as hybrids connected to a source of renewable energy (for example, the Gannawarra solar-cum-battery) or to support network operations (as with the Ballarat system). AGL further claimed to invest in a total of 850MW of storage capacity, to be introduced into the NEM by 2024. TransGrid also announced it was investing in a large-scale battery to provide frequency-response services and 'synthetic' inertia.

In the face of these investments and the new reality of batteries, AEMO submitted a substantial rule-change request to the AEMC in October 2020 to better accommodate storage. This rule-change request is a start but it is timid in the face of the enormous work required to integrate storage into the grid. In fact we know very little of the economics of grid-scale storage; the only solid research of reference (Karaduman 2020) warns us that the merchant model of energy arbitrage is not financially viable at current costs. Indeed, the Hornsdale battery derives most of its income from the FCAS market rather than by arbitraging prices in the energy market. Likewise, the investment in the Big Battery in Victoria rests on a capacity payment from the state of Victoria for five-sixths of its capacity. Hence there exists a distinct risk, as has occurred with merchant transmission, to see the enthusiasm of investors evaporate.[15]

Storage integration in the grid of the NEM is full of promises, as well as challenges. The promises of storage are, first, a better 'coincidence of wants'. Electricity produced in periods of low demand (and so not worth much) can be made available in high-demand periods, when it is more valuable. This alone makes storage a very good complement to intermittent electricity generation. Second, Variable Renewable Energy (VRE) generators may be classified as dispatchable ('scheduled') if seconded by a storage unit. Third, electricity can be made subject to (intertemporal) price arbitrage. Thus, storage can smooth prices as well as production. Fourth, in doing so, storage can be used, by NSPs for example, to alleviate congestion on the network. Fifth, thanks to their almost immediate response times, batteries are very adept at managing frequency control, and may even be an acceptable substitute to declining system inertia. Finally, through its energy arbitrage activities, storage may engender a new degree of competition on the generation side. To take full advantage of this opportunity, however, one should make sure storage units are not owned – at least not in large numbers – by incumbent generators and 'gen-tailers', and that storage units do not become too large.[16]

---

15   This being written with the caveat that the cost of storage keeps falling, unlike that of transmission investment.

16   There are no returns to scale in storage, which is a constant-return-to-scale technology, hence no social benefit to scale. However, there is a risk of unilateral exercise of market power, which is socially costly.

Storage brings its own set of challenges too. First, a storage unit can either charge or discharge at almost any point in time, so it is (at any given time) either a load or a source of energy. The ability to do either implies the market operator must distinguish between bids to buy and bids to sell. Given bids, it must then decide how to dispatch the storage entity upon the market clearing. That is, if a unit simultaneously bid to buy or sell (at different prices), is it then dispatched as a load or a generator? This decision may depend on the clearing price, the conditions of supply and demand, the congestion on the grid, the expectations of the dispatcher about the future, and possibly other factors. Further, the ability of a storage unit to charge and discharge depends on its current state of charge; its (marginal) cost depends on the sequence of past decisions to charge and discharge, and its incentives depend on current prices and its expectations over future prices. In other words, a storage operator explicitly engages in a *dynamic stochastic game*, with a marginal cost that is endogenous to this game. This is a new behaviour that is not currently encoded in the market design in Australia; that is, the current bidding and clearing rules are not adequate to these rich, dynamic strategies. Furthermore, the state of charge of any one battery is a critical variable to this game. Should it be disclosed, monitored, or can the market operator afford to remain ignorant of its true value?

Storage can also be used in conjunction with other assets. For example, it can be coupled to a VRE plant to firm it up and so turn it into a dispatchable load; it can supply critical frequency control and voltage control services that become increasingly demanded as VRE penetration continues; it can supply a substitute to the natural inertia of rotating generators, which are being progressively retired. These opportunities raise new questions. How does one value these complementary services? For example, at present, there is no market for inertia, which is freely supplied by the rotating masses of thermal generators. While there is a market for FCAS, how these services are valued is in fact not clear. As demonstrated by TransGrid, network operators may wish to invest in storage to protect their network assets as net demand becomes more volatile. Should one allow network operators to buy and sell energy? Should there be a cap to battery capacity for network assets in order to adhere to the structural separation of the industry? Or should this investment not be allowed, in which case network operators would have to rely on third parties to invest in storage and contract with them? Further, if batteries can be used to store the excess capacity of renewable generators (as in Table 2 above), at what price should this energy be purchased upon charging? In the example of Table 2, the value of a marginal unit of energy is zero in the market. But if a storage operator anticipates to sell it at a positive price in the future, is it free to negotiate a transaction price with the generator in a bilateral contract, should a market be organised for these transactions too, or should they simply occur in the wholesale pool?

Next, because storage plays a *dynamic* game, dispatching becomes also a dynamic problem. As was shown in the examples of section *D*, the very notion of merit order changes in a dynamic problem. Nowadays, the merit order is simple: modulo dispatch constraints, the lower bidders are dispatched in full first, irrespective of what to expect in the future. With a dynamic problem, the determination of the merit order depends on the time horizon – as in Table 2. In addition, dispatching storage to discharge at time t means it is no longer available (to discharge) at $t+k$, $k \geq 1$, and conversely of course. This problem does not exist with generators: a generator that produces at t can also produce at $t+k$. It is extremely unlikely that a sequence of static (hence, myopic) optima can replicate the sequence of optimal dispatches that solve the dynamic problem. It certainly does not in the example of Tables 1 and 2. Hence a new dispatch engine is likely required, to solve a problem no one knows how to formulate yet.

Finally, day-ahead markets likely have a role to play in accommodating storage integration because they allow for systematic intertemporal arbitrage. The firm schedules of day-ahead markets feature *certain* price differences that storage can exploit to generate the revenue it needs to sustain itself. Indeed, in California for example, 100% of price differences between peak demand and minimum demand are strictly positive (Wolak 2029). That is, a storage operator can generate a *certain* revenue simply by blindly buying at the trough and selling at the peak; this is the dream of any arbitrageur. The quantum of this revenue determines the extent of the storage investment.

In closing, integrating storage into the grid requires a thorough redesign of the market rules, as well as revisiting questions of industrial organisation.

4. Reserve mechanisms and capacity markets

Reserves seem to have crept to the forefront of the policy debate in the last few years. Maybe having reserves is a reassuring notion; it is also very expensive. This renewed interest in reserves and reserve markets is surprising because significant incidents on the grid are typically induced by network outages, rather than supply shortages – as, for example, the islanding of South Australia in 2016. Even the Callide explosion of May 2021 did not trigger anything else than a temporary shortage of power – but a significant network event.

In the NEM, reserves may come in two forms: load reserves or generating reserves. The Reliability and Emergency Trader (RERT) mechanism used by AEMO is essentially a load reserve mechanism, whereby loads are contracted in advance by AEMO to decrease their consumption when the system comes under stress. In return these loads are paid a compensation that is contractually agreed on.

Real-time pricing, together with an elastic demand function, achieve the same result. Indeed, loads that elect to reduce consumption for a return would also reduce their consumption if the price of energy were immediately reflected, and if they had that flexibility.[17] To see that, simply observe that, for a load, the decrease in value from reducing energy use from q_1 to q_2 must be no more than the agreed transfer they receive under RERT. This is the usual equilibrium condition: marginal cost is no more than marginal benefit. In the other direction, it is equivalent to saying that the marginal benefit of increasing energy use from q_2 to q_1 is lower than the marginal cost. That marginal cost to the load is $p_1q_1-p_2q_2$: the revenue difference paid out by loads to generators. With an appropriate market design, in which the demand side is elastic, these indifference conditions can be exactly expressed by loads. In other words, a reserve mechanism like the RERT may only be necessary because the normal economic forces are stifled in the current institutional design. At least, even if costly, the RERT – and mechanisms like it – have the benefit of providing relief in the system because they induce a decrease in consumption, which is not always the case.

Reserves, and reserve markets, in generating capacity, are much more problematic. The problem with this kind of reserves is this. Absent any entry by a new generator, there is a fixed total capacity to produce energy; setting aside generating reserves decreases the available capacity, with two effects. First, it contributes to increasing the clearing price in the spot energy market simply because less capacity can bid to supply. Therefore, even if reserves are not called upon, prices are higher for *all* participants. Second, reserves are called in when demand exceeds available capacity, which is much more likely to occur now that available capacity is reduced by the amount of the reserves. When called upon, these reserves are (typically) sold at the prevailing spot price, which is very high then. It is quite transparent that the creation of generating reserves (and markets) does not increase capacity. Rather, it creates an artificial shortage that justifies the purchase of reserves at a price

---

17   Moving to a 5-minute settlement will help in enhancing the responsiveness of the scheduled load.

that exceeds what would be the market-clearing price. Here too, real-time pricing with an elastic demand function performs better and at a much lower social cost – provided the price cap is high enough.

To see why, consider the following toy model; it is stark but instructive. The induced supply function is $S(p)=p$ and there may be a high-demand state with demand $D(p)=2-p$ and a low-demand state with $D(p)=1-p$. It is trivial to verify that the clearing prices and quantities are $(p^H=1, q^H=1)$ and $(p^L=1/2, q^L=1/2)$. Thus, if capacity is $K=1$, the equilibrium demand can always be served; if the cost of capacity is not too high it is installed and available to use when required. Suppose now the market operator reserves half this capacity. In the low-demand state this has no consequence: capacity $K=1/2$ is just sufficient to meet $q^L=1/2$. As the system moves to the high demand state, the clearing price jumps to $p^H=3/2$ while the quantity remains 1/2, whereupon the market operator releases an additional 1/2 of quantity *at the prevailing price* of 3/2. Hence the total generator revenue in the high-demand state increases from 1 to 3/2 (50% more).

It is not surprising that generators like reserve markets. For consumers they are at best a mirage. They are also a good example of the unintended consequences of market interference. Markets are best when they are carefully designed, but then left to their own devices to run.

References

Allaz, B. and Jean-Luc Vila (1993). 'Cournot competition, forward markets and efficiency', *Journal of Economic Theory* 59, 1–16.

Birchler, M., Vladimir Fux and Jacob Goeree (2019). 'Designing combinatorial exchanges for the reallocation of resource rights', *PNAS* 116(3), 786–791.

Gans, J. and Frank Wolak (2007). 'A comparison of ex ante versus ex post vertical market power: Evidence from the electricity supply industry', *working paper*, Stanford University.

Karaduman, O. (2020). 'The economics of grid-scale storage', *working paper*, MIT Economics.

Leslie, G., Armin Poukhanali and Guillaume Roger (2021). 'Can real-time pricing be progressive? Identifying cross-subsidies under fixed-rate electricity tariffs', *working paper*, Monash University.

Lindsay, L. and Jacob Goere (2020). 'The exposure problem and market design', *The Review of Economic Studies* 87(5), 2230–2255.

Newberry, D. (1995). 'Power markets and market power', *The Energy Journal* 16(3), 39–66.

Roger, G. (2018). 'An economic analysis of the National Electricity Market', Technical report for *Energy Consumers Australia*.

Wolak, F. (2004). 'Managing unilateral market power in electricity', *working paper*, Stanford University.

CPSIA information can be obtained
at www.ICGtesting.com
Printed in the USA
JSHW050423300123
36871JS00004B/23

9 781922 633217